PATRIARCHAL STRUCTURES
IN SHAKESPEARE'S DRAMA

PATRIARCHAL STRUCTURES IN SHAKESPEARE'S DRAMA

PETER ERICKSON

University of California Press

Berkeley
Los Angeles
London

University of California Press
Berkeley and Los Angeles, California
University of California Press, Ltd.
London, England
© 1985 by
The Regents of the University of California

Library of Congress Cataloging in Publication Data
Erickson, Peter.
Patriarchal structures in Shakespeare's drama.
Includes index.
1. Shakespeare, William, 1564–1616—Political and
social views.   2. Patriarchy in literature.   3. Men in
literature.   4. Family in literature.   5. Social struc-
ture in literature.   6. Sex role in literature.   I. Title.
PR3024.E7 1985   822.3'3   84-601
ISBN 0-520-04806-7

Printed in the United States of America
1   2   3   4   5   6   7   8   9

For Tay
and for
Andrew, Ingrid,
and Benjamin

Contents

Preface

This study is concerned with the literary representation of gender and with the political implications of that representation in particular plays. Love often affects men and women differently in Shakespeare's drama, and these differences lead to an asymmetry in the distribution of power, whose practical consequences shape a play's overall social structure and hence our sense of the outcome. The value of sexual politics as a critical concept is that it draws attention to this conjunction of love and power, allowing us to ask questions about characters' relative power. Does the range of options for male and female roles in a given play promote mutuality and equality, or does it foster a disparity that favors one sex at the expense of the other? And what do the answers to these questions reveal about the dynamic of the play as a whole?

As such questions imply, Shakespeare's drama has a social dimension that must be directly addressed. Characters in a specific play can be viewed from three perspectives: the development of an individual character; the relationships between characters; and, finally, the way characters as a group collectively constitute a social and cultural entity, which individual characters can decisively shape but which also shapes those characters and acts as a force that constrains their development and their relationships. While continuing to respect the importance of the first two perspectives, we should not neglect the significance of the third. A play's social dimension is not limited to institutions and formal hierarchy. Even more pertinent are the relatively informal modes to which we gain access through close reading: emotions, actions, gestures, improvisations, assumptions, expectations, and, above all, rhetorical patterns and language. To describe "a particular sense of life, a particular community of experience hardly needing expression" that he seeks in analyzing an entire culture, Raymond Williams chooses the phrase *structure of feeling:* "It is as firm and definite as 'structure' suggests, yet it operates in the most delicate and least tangible parts of our activity."[1] This concept of a "structure of feeling" can be applied to individual plays and used to assess the sexual political configuration of a given dramatic situation.

My interpretation focuses primarily on dramatic texts and on the versions of society that emerge in them. Nevertheless, there is a connection between these fictional microcosms and the external historical context. The patriarchal structures that I derive from close analysis of the plays themselves coincide with the "reinforcement of patriarchy" that Lawrence Stone identifies as a central organizing principle in the period in which Shakespeare is writing.[2] Stone sees a parallel emergence of the nation-state and the nuclear family because both these political forms place a similar stress on obedience:

> The growth of paternalism was deliberately encouraged by the new Renaissance state on the traditional grounds that the subordination of the family to its head is analogous to, and also a direct contributory cause of, subordination of subjects to the sovereign. . . . The state, therefore, had a direct interest in reinforcing patriarchy in the home.[3]

Shakespeare gives extraordinary play to this interdependence between royal and family politics by making them converge in a royal family—an intensification dramatized to an acute degree in *King Lear*. A social system whose authority is vested in a father has a highly charged resonance in Shakespeare; whether weak or strong, the paternal figure is a chief point of reference for the characters. Moreover, the overlapping of family politics and sexual politics in Shakespeare's drama provides a focal point for the analysis of gender and gives the term *patriarchal* its interpretive force.

My greatest debts are to my teachers C. L. Barber and Harry Berger, Jr., both of whom supervised my dissertation on *Henry V* at the University of California, Santa Cruz. The complicated intellectual heritage I received from them was further enriched by my friendship with each mentor; the strength of these bonds has helped to sustain my work well beyond graduate school. Barber died in March 1980 as this book began to take shape and as I was completing essays on *As You Like It* and *The Winter's Tale* that were to become draft versions of the book's first and final chapters. In the essay that concludes *Shakespeare's "Rough Magic": Essays in Honor of C. L. Barber*, I have had the opportunity to give a fuller tribute to his impact. While writing this book, I have been aware how often he remains my first audience; I trust that he would accept the book, despite our differences of interpretation.

I first met Harry Berger in his role as Spenserian. Coming from an undergraduate literary education in which I had been unable to break the spell F. R. Leavis had cast over *The Faerie Queene*,[4] I was astonished by Berger's ability to bring the text to life and especially by his acuity in reading the poem's landscapes and situations as symbolic manifestations of the heroes' internal psychological development. I have never encountered a more spirited, tenacious, and fiercely hard-working teacher, nor one for whom research and teaching are more closely allied and mutually reinforcing. He has a remarkable capacity to bring the full force and complexity of his interpretation into the classroom and, without sacrificing or diluting its sophistication, to make it available to students. I have learned from Berger's exceptional courage in asking and pursuing difficult questions.

I have also been heartened by conversations with a number of younger Shakespeareans, chief among them Janet Adelman, Shirley Garner, Madelon Gohlke, Coppélia Kahn, and Richard Wheeler. Individually, they have given me either valuable confirmation of my experience with the texts or lively disagreement. Both kinds of response provided the human context that enabled me to grow. My work on this book was framed by year-long stays at two graduate centers. In 1967–68, supported by an Amherst College Memorial Fellowship, I studied at the Centre for Contemporary Cultural Studies at the University of Birmingham in England. I trace my interest in sexual roles to a collective project there, led by Stuart Hall, on images of women in short stories from popular women's magazines. In 1981–82, a Kent Fellowship, co-sponsored by Wesleyan University and the Society for Values in Higher Education, allowed me to pursue my own work and to imbibe the concentrated intellectual energy of Wesleyan's Center for the Humanities.

At the University of California Press, Doris Kretschmer, my editor, and Estelle Jelinek, copyeditor, have given invaluable help at various stages in the process of preparing the manuscript for publication. As the typist of the final manuscript, Patricia Camden of Wesleyan's Center for the Humanities has been unfailing in her efficiency, kindness, and good humor.

Earlier versions of Chapters 1 and 5 appeared, respectively, in *Massachusetts Review* 23 (1982): 65–83; and *PMLA* 97 (1982): 819–29. The citations to Shakespeare's works are from *The Riverside Shakespeare*, ed. G. Blakemore Evans (Boston: Houghton Mifflin, 1974).

Introduction

A central element in the analysis of gender in Shakespeare's drama concerns the way relationships between men and women are complicated by coexistence with strong ties between men. The conflict between male–female relations and male–male relations is a pervasive motif in Shakespeare's drama; his treatment of it, however, is not uniform. He explores a variety of possible outcomes, ranging from resolutions that endorse marital love, to those that favor male bonds, to those that remain ambiguously divided between these two contending alternatives. Where marriage is successful, it must overcome or mitigate male bonds that have behind them the force of patriarchal social norms.[1] The basic conflict is constant, but the particular constellation in which it originates and to which it leads varies considerably from play to play. The issue of male bonding gives no license to reduce the plays to a single, repeated formula. On the contrary, the variety is proof against such reductionism.

At the same time, this diversity is not an aesthetic end in itself, as though Shakespeare had arbitrarily chosen an explosive theme and gratuitously manipulated it solely for artistic effect, while standing above it all, neutral and indifferent. Rather, the energy and excitement of his artistic dexterity come from his power to create multiple perspectives on matters in which he can be assumed to have had an emotional stake. Shakespeare is not trapped in a fixed dramatic formula of male bonding; instead he is able to use the medium of drama for sustained critical exploration. His artistic freedom implies authorial growth.[2] The concept of Shakespeare's chronological development, to which I am committed, means that his variety, though important, is not infinite, but forms a distinct pattern, however provisional we must be in formulating it.

Although it is neither possible nor desirable to reduce Shakespeare's entire corpus to a schematic grid, it is useful for introductory purposes to speak in abstract terms of a trend in his work as a whole. In his early work, Shakespeare presents male characters who powerfully resist women. The two characteristic expressions of this resistance are desperately simple: either avoiding women altogether as Talbot does in *1 Henry VI* or, like Richard III, warding them off through denigration and caricature. This hostility to women can usually be seen as an attempt to cover up a fear of women that the male character is emotionally ill-equipped to confront and from which he takes refuge in a male friendship, group, or activity. Even combat with other men is more comforting and secure than dealing with women. The contrast between male friendship and male rivalry is not absolute, and the concept of male bonding encompasses both. Aggressive relationships are a special case of male bonding because of an intimate involvement with the rival that can have a mirroring effect. First, the rival must be carefully chosen: he must have sufficient stature to be worthy of combat and sufficient prominence to ensure that his defeat enhances the victor's prestige. Second, as Prince Hal's final tribute to the dying Hotspur shows, more than formal respect is at issue: the other side of rivalrous hate is a certain fondness and affection, though Hal reveals these feelings only when his triumph makes it safe to do so—and even then his manner is guarded.

The aspiration toward a masculine purity based on the exclusion of women is linked to the general contradiction in Renaissance culture between the ideal of the whole man and the dichotomization of woman,[3] an inherently tragic contradiction since male wholeness depends ultimately on an integrated view of women. The strategy of protecting men from contamination by dividing women into two groups—those who can be trusted and those who cannot—only exacerbates the problem it tries to solve. Such classification makes all women suspect because men can never be sure that they have correctly categorized a woman. Moreover, the preoccupation with an external split into good and bad women masks an unresolved interior split between "masculine" and "feminine" facets of the male self. The rigid separation of masculine and feminine and the systematic suppression of the latter, held to be essential to a secure male identity, are counterproductive. The separation prevents fruitful coordination of masculine and feminine elements, thereby blocking psychic wholeness in the male. The action in the tragedies may be played primarily in terms of the destruction of the woman, but it is always accompanied by the self-destruction of the male hero.

Over the course of Shakespeare's career, however, there is a gradual shift toward a possible accommodation with women; and eventually, accompanied by struggle and anguish, more positive forms of association begin to emerge. One reason for this shift is the need to come to terms with the family as the unit of reproduction, a need expressed with largely negative results by the destructive urgency of the tragic period. The task becomes not reconciliation with women in general, but reconciliation with women as mothers, the mother who gave birth to the male protagonist or the potential mother of his children. The opening sonnets on procreation testify to the difficulty of encountering this specific version of the threat women present. The sonnets advising the young man to take a wife seem to advocate family continuity in the most benign and attractive terms. Yet the rest of the sonnets turn defensively from this prospect, flying from it with a counterproposal of male love. For a moment, the poet protests that the two means to immortality are compatible—"But were some child of yours alive that time, / You should live twice, in it and in my rhyme" (17.13–14)—and that his art is the weaker—"And fortify yourself in your decay / With a means more blessed than my barren rhyme" (16.3–4). But this moment rapidly gives way to an assertion of the supremacy of artistic power, in which procreation disappears except insofar as its imagery has been taken over by the artist's "ingrafting" (15.14): "So long lives this, and this gives life to thee" (18.14).

For male characters readily haunted by female (particularly maternal) betrayal, images of a trustworthy and forgiving mother prove elusive, and a plausible mother figure is not staged until Hermione's appearance at the end of *The Winter's Tale*. However, male–male relations in Shakespeare's work are not ultimately replaced through simple substitution by male–female relations as the emotional center of his dramatic worlds. On the contrary, ties between men remain central. Shakespeare's final version, manifested in *The Winter's Tale,* is to have it both ways. The two claims of allegiance to the man (and to the patriarchal power structure) and of allegiance to the woman are balanced against each other, preventing either from becoming too all-encompassing. Even at this late point in Shakespeare's career, the male character's bonds with men and with women are not totally compatible or harmonized; the sense of competing modes of relationship remains.

The concept *male bonding* here describes relations that form the basis for male-oriented institutions within the plays. The term *homosexual* is avoided as an automatic characterization of the physical component of male bonds in order to distinguish between the explicitly sexual relationship and the attraction that is part of male camaraderie. The poet's relationship to the young man in the *Sonnets* provides a model that is often consistent with male ties elsewhere in Shakespeare's work. The erotic intensity of the poet's apprehension of the beloved is accompanied neither by homosexual consummation nor even, according to the last four lines of sonnet 20, by sexual desire. The youth's attractiveness can be celebrated because it is free of the drive for sexual gratification that is directed toward the woman. Similarly, in *As You Like It* male solidarity in the forest includes the expression of physical affection in the form of nurturant feeding, that is, in an oral rather than genital form. The security of male bodies mirroring and confirming a common physical identity depends precisely on relief from the specifically genital demand associated with the opposite sex.

However, in other instances, the rhetoric is so overt that it enacts a verbal consummation. In *Coriolanus*, male comrades transfer the language of heterosexual love to themselves with such enthusiasm that the marital bond that provides the analogy seems to pale:

> O! let me clip ye
> In arms as sound as when I woo'd, in heart
> As merry as when our nuptial day was done
> And tapers burnt to bedward!
> (1.6.29–32)

> Know thou first,
> I lov'd the maid I married; never man
> Sigh'd truer breath; but that I see thee here,
> Thou noble thing, more dances my rapt heart
> Than when I first my wedded mistress saw
> Bestride my threshold. . . .
> I have nightly since
> Dreamt of encounters 'twixt thyself and me;
> We have been down together in my sleep,
> Unbuckling helms, fisting each other's throat.
> (4.5.113–18, 122–25)

In such moments eroticized violence between men becomes transparent.[4] Although the military context assures that manliness has not been abrogated, war becomes an occasion for sexual contact. How thin this indirection can become is suggested by the mutual death of York and Suffolk in *Henry V*. One model for male interaction will not suffice; sonnet 20 cannot be used to draw the line everywhere in Shakespeare. We must see a range of physical behavior between men and try to make distinctions within that range. But the question of the exact physical status of a particular male bond is not the only question.

The sexual question should not be overemphasized so that it diverts attention from other, more significant aspects of male bonding. The main focus here is on the political and psychological implications of male ties as the basis for patriarchal power by which men control women, whether ruthlessly or benevolently. The key issue to be addressed is the tendency of male characters to have primary attachment and loyalty to men rather than to women. Male bonding speaks to the striking political and emotional investment men make in one another and considers the physical component as an adjunct rather than the principal motive or cause of this investment.

If the label *homosexual* is oversimplified in one direction, then the other side of a sexual/spiritual dichotomy is even less satisfactory. As applied to male ties in the plays, the terms *spiritual* and *Platonic* are ethereal and bland to the point of distorting the rich material with which we must come to grips. The spiritual explanation—or the related contention that male friendship should be understood as merely a familiar Renaissance convention that need concern us no further—treats male bonds as if they existed in a vacuum, as though the plays did not surround them with a dramatic situation and a social context that help to shape the meaning of those bonds. Male–male relationships are pursued in Shakespeare's drama primarily through sublimated rather than directly homosexual forms: the argument concerns the nature of the sublimation. A spiritual emphasis cannot do justice to the psychological force and political consequences of male ties and hence minimizes or explains away their crucial importance. Male bonding accurately insists on this psychological and political domain, which neither term in the sexual/spiritual duality adequately characterizes.

Because I view male bonds in Shakespeare's work as an obstacle to relations between men and women, my analysis seems to give the concept *male bonding* an overall negative cast. However, beyond the specific situation of Shakespeare's work I do not subscribe to a system in which relationships between men are considered abnormal and heterosexual relations normal. In the present context, however, there are two negative elements built into male associations. First, male bonding is linked to patriarchal political institutions by means of which male characters establish and maintain domination. Second, an antifeminist attitude, whether manifested as overt debasement or understated co-option, is routinely incorporated into male bonds in the plays under discussion. These conditions are not universally present in male bonds, but they do prevent an uncritical, idealized view of male–male relations in the case of Shakespeare.

Finally, an explanation is in order for focusing on male–male relations and male–female relations without an equivalent emphasis on relations between women. This neglect is a function of the configuration that Shakespeare offers: the specific material at hand gives insufficient weight to female bonds to make it a motif equal in importance to the other two. In theory, the term *bonding* ought to apply to same-sex relations for both men and women. In the actual situation, however, the possibilities for female bonds are severely restricted. Relations between women are present either as lost opportunities—as in the case of Gertrude's elegy for Ophelia—or as subsidiary events peripheral to the male-centered action—as in the case of the brief reunion of Hermione and Perdita where the full potency of the Ceres–Proserpina analogue and its connection to the Eleusinian mysteries are obscured. Similarly, the bond between Hermione and Paulina is kept largely off-stage: it is not dramatized in and of itself as a central relationship, as demonstrated in act 2, scene 2, where the two women make contact only through an intermediary. More generally, female intimacy is treated as an adolescent phase that will naturally be superseded by courtship. Fervent declarations by young women of their oneness with each other are never accorded full seriousness. Because such fervor is seen unquestionably as temporary, it is tolerated with bemused indulgence. Helena and Hermia in *A Midsummer Night's Dream* and Rosalind and Celia in *As You Like It* are examples of female ties that are sundered by the marital action of the play.[5] Similar expectations are not as a matter of course insisted upon for male characters, for whom marriage does not necessarily preclude continued strong bonds with men. In practice, men have two major channels for relationships whereas women are allowed only the heterosexual option. Emilia's moving assertion of allegiance to Desdemona under extreme provocation in the final scene of *Othello* is an exception that reinforces the general rule of the strict suppression or subordination of female alliances. Refusing obedience to her husband, Emilia joins Desdemona in death: "O, lay me by my mistress' side" (5.2.237). But her place in "the tragic loading of this bed" (363) is not assured since it remains uncertain whether her request is honored and since the final disposition of Desdemona's body belongs to Othello, who "dies upon a kiss" (359).

As if female bonding poses a potential challenge so dangerous and subversive that it would be impossible to keep under control, Shakespeare's usual procedure is, effectively, not to permit female ties to become fully developed in the first place so that they will never become equal in strength or scope to male bonds.[6] The logical conclusion of this defense is epitomized by Miranda's isolation as a woman. Having been deprived of the "four, or five, women once that tended me" (*Tempest*, 1.2.47), she lacks a same-sex model with whom she could identify and use as the basis for constructing a female self: "I do not know / One of my sex; no woman's face remember, / Save, from my glass, mine own" (3.1.48–50).

Now let us turn to an overview of my analyses of the individual plays that are the substance of this study.

In *Love's Labor's Lost*, aspirations to immortality, echoing the war against time in the sonnets to the young man, take the form of a commitment to male bonding that explicitly renounces women. This isolationist impulse is mocked but is conspicuously not replaced by marital ties. The awkward ending can be seen as the product of an uneasy stasis in which neither male ties nor heterosexual bonds are affirmed. The play thus exhibits in a stark, rudimentary way the problematic tension between the two. As in *Venus and Adonis*, the surface tone of humor and facetiousness is insufficient to dispel the fundamental anxiety the play communicates. In contrast to *Love's Labor's Lost*, in which the marital culmination, if forthcoming at all, must be optimistically imagined as occurring outside the bounds of the play, *As You Like It* ostentatiously enacts the promise (especially for the main couple) of marital success. However, the competing motif of male bonding does not disappear but survives intact. The all-male communion in the forest presided over by Duke Senior is recapitulated at the play's end by the restoration of his patriarchal authority and by the denial of female presence in the Epilogue where Rosalind is discovered to be a boy actor. The formal achievement of *As You Like It* lies not in its elimination of the appeal of male bonding, but rather in its more sophisticated manner of managing both sides of the tension between male ties and heterosexual union.

The exclusive commitment to male relations, made laughable in *Love's Labor's Lost*, is taken seriously in *Henry*

V where the idea of a pure male realm, transferred from pastoral to historical space, is given compelling (though not unqualified) dramatization. Ferdinand's "sweet fellowship in shame" (*LLL*, 4.3.47) is transformed into Henry V's stirring appeal to "fellowship" prior to Agincourt: "We few, we happy few, we band of brothers" (*H5*, 4.3.39, 60). But if the death scene of York and Suffolk narrated in act 4, scene 6, shows how far Shakespeare could go toward a sentimental portrait of male bonds, the frame device also suggests his capacity for critical perspective. The insularity of male warfare is disrupted slightly when women are hastily introduced for the finale. But Henry V's prolonged wooing is made to seem a mechanical final step in the completion of an all-around man, which only confirms how severely limited he is by the one-sided martial identity that he repeatedly proffers to Katherine: "Will you vouchsafe to teach a soldier terms, / Such as will enter at a lady's ear?" (5.2.99–100). The festive expectations aroused by the politically enforced marriage are left unfulfilled not only because the Epilogue appends a cautionary note about subsequent historical developments, but more importantly because Henry V is felt to be locked into the narrow masculinity he has displayed throughout the play.

Viewed as sequels to *Henry V*, *Hamlet* and *Othello* sharply raise the stakes. While Henry V's heroic career is feebly extended by his anticlimactic encounter with a woman, *Hamlet* and *Othello* place the male hero's ambivalent relationship with women at the center of attention. When this relationship becomes intolerable, the hero finds solace in a pact with a man. Turning away from Ophelia, Hamlet turns toward Horatio, who loyally agrees to tell Hamlet's story. Othello collaborates with Iago in the struggle to overthrow his belief in Desdemona's honesty: "I think my wife be honest, and think she is not" (3.3.384). The delusion that Othello tries to substitute for his belief is fostered by the instinctive logic that a man is automatically to be more trusted than a woman, above all in moments of extreme crisis. Since Othello's perception is so exactly the reverse of the truth the audience painfully possesses, the play bitterly exposes the bankruptcy of male bonding. Hamlet uses his male companion for different purposes, but the outcome for women is similar. Though Hamlet strains against the heroic masculinity defined by revenge convention as Othello embraces it, Hamlet nonetheless shares Othello's misogynist rhetoric. Like Othello, Hamlet subjects his woman to a catechism on her honesty—"are you honest?" (3.1.102)—which helps to destroy her. The accusation is so rigged that Ophelia is deprived in advance of any chance to refute it; the case against her is air-tight because it is a generic one: "Frailty, thy name is woman!" (1.2.146). *King Lear* reduces the hold of male bonding. Lear's determined reliance on the male group that comforts him on the heath is undercut by its limited efficacy. These male ties cannot compensate for the loss of Cordelia, and the play moves resolutely toward a positive appreciation of her frailty. Nonetheless, this appreciation is compromised by the use Lear makes of it to reinstate paternal control.

Antony and Cleopatra displays a more tolerant, if not entirely accepting, attitude toward the frailties of both men and women. The male protagonist's attachment to reputation, the loss of which so concerns Cassio and Othello, is drastically diminished, loosened, and finally let go. To a far greater degree than Othello, Antony is preoccupied with the "new heaven, new earth" (1.1.17) that a woman seems to have revealed to him, a revelation that Antony's intermittent attacks of jealousy are not permitted permanently to obscure. *Antony and Cleopatra* makes a decisive break with the convention of male bonding. Antony's relationship with Enobarbus is kept distinctly secondary to the fundamental commitment to Cleopatra. However poignant their separation, it is Enobarbus rather than Antony who is left to mourn the loss of their friendship and to suffer for it. Antony's gesture of returning his friend's treasure is simply one in a series of magnanimous acts by which he divests himself of "all th' addition" to a military hero until he reaches the point where he can set aside "the name" as well: "No more a soldier" (4.14.42). The question of what kind of masculine identity Antony has once he is no longer a soldier is of course a complex one. Though the power of male bonding has lost its hold on Antony, the claims of traditional manliness are reasserted at the end of the play through the military success of Octavius.

The Winter's Tale is perhaps Shakespeare's most explicit dramatization of the tension between male bonds and heterosexual ties. The play's opening highlights Polixenes's vision of pursuing male friendship in the absence of women. This obstacle to heterosexual bonds is ultimately counteracted by a reconciliation of men and women unprecedented in Shakespeare's work. The sequence of Leontes's responses to the statue in the final scene reenacts the process of courtship, as though Leontes must literally woo the statue in order to relearn and reexperience heterosexual desire. The spectacular form of the restoration of Hermione and consequently of marital fulfillment can be seen as a measure of the force that is needed to overcome the initial homoerotic ideal announced by Polixenes.

Shakespeare's drama registers an astonishing growth in his male characters' capacity to imagine and to engage in constructive relations with women. At the same time, it is important to stress that this achievement has distinct limits. The general formulation that emerges from this analysis hinges on a contrast between crude and benign forms of patriarchy. This distinction corresponds to the two definitions of individual masculine identity that Eugene Waith describes as available in the Renaissance.[7] The characteristic movement away from violent toward humane patriarchy as a play unfolds provides a measure for the growth of male characters and for the standards to which their author holds them. Yet a balanced assessment is suggested because benevolent patriarchy, despite its merits, is not without its problematic side; it cannot be mistaken for the attainment of fully independent female characters.

1

Sexual Politics and Social Structure
in *As You Like It*

The dramatic and emotional effect of Shakespearean comedy can be defined as a process of making manifest "a tough reasonableness beneath the slight lyric grace."[1] This comic toughness derives in part from Shakespeare's ability to mix genres, an ability that helps to account for his artistic power.[2] In exploring Shakespeare's use of genre, we must be concerned as much with overlapping as with differentiation. The father–son motif, for example, provides a specific point of contact between *As You Like It* and *Henry V*. The analogous relationships between Duke Senior and Orlando in the first play and Henry IV and Hal in the second help to cut across an oversimplified generic distinction that says history plays deal with political power (implicitly understood as male power) whereas comedies treat love. Rosalind's androgynous allure can appear so attractive, her linguistic virtuosity so engaging, that all our attention becomes focused on her, as if nothing else happened or mattered. Her talking circles around Orlando seems sufficient proof of her complete triumph. Yet this line of response is deficient because it ignores important parts of the play; that is, political power is a significant element in *As You Like It*.

The transmission of paternal heritage, announced at the outset in Orlando's lament, begins to receive fulfillment when Orlando fashions an alliance with Duke Senior in the forest when no women are present. After his initial complaint about being deprived of a "good education" (1.1.67–68), Orlando is educated twice: once by Rosalind's father and then by Rosalind. The exiles in the forest can indulge in the pleasures of melancholy because the play can amply satisfy the need for true versions of debased human relationship: "Most friendship is feigning, most loving mere folly" (2.7.181). We relish the platitude of this general rule in order to appreciate the magic of the exceptions. But the question still remains: how are the twin themes of friendship and loving coordinated with each other? And an exclusive focus on Rosalind prevents our asking it. Male friendship, exemplified by the reconciliation of Duke Senior and Orlando, provides a framework that diminishes and contains Rosalind's apparent power. My point is not that *As You Like It* is a history play in disguise or that there are no differences between genres. The pastoral feast in the forest of Arden is far less stressful than the feast of Crispian that Henry V imagines as an antidote to the disturbing memory of his inheritance through "the fault / My father made in compassing the crown" (*H5*, 4.1.293–94). Unlike Henry V, Orlando is never made to confront a paternal fault. However, an exaggerated contrast between history and comedy is misleading. Concentration on Rosalind to the neglect of other issues distorts the overall design of *As You Like It*, one that is governed by male ends.

I

The endings of *Love's Labor's Lost* and *As You Like It* present a striking contrast. In the earlier play, Berowne comments explicitly on the absence of marriage and closure, for which, in his frustration, he holds the women responsible: "Our wooing doth not end like an old play: / Jack hath not Gill. These ladies' courtesy / Might well have made our sport a comedy" (5.2.874–76). *Love's Labor's Lost* culminates in the failure of courtship, but *As You Like It* reaches a fully and flamboyantly festive conclusion with the onstage revelation of the symbol of marital union, Hymen, who presides over a quadruple wedding. The prevailing mood of sourness at the end of *Love's Labor's Lost* is held in check in the later play by confining the potential for bitterness and disruption to Jaques, the nonparticipant. But even Jaques generously acknowledges the validity of love when he gives his blessing to Orlando, whom he had formerly mocked as "Signior Love" (3.2.292): "You to a love, that your true faith doth merit" (5.4.188).

In the final scene of *Love's Labor's Lost*, festivity is short-circuited. The concluding masques and songs are no more helpful in facilitating the happy ending than the men's poetry had been earlier. The masques of the Muscovites and of the Nine Worthies are farcical artistic performances that precipitate discord. "More Ates, more Ates! stir them on, stir them on!" (5.2.688–89), cries Berowne in an enthusiastic effort to provoke violence between Costard and Armado. Nor do the companion songs of the cuckoo and the owl dispel the awkward atmosphere. The songs act as a conspicuously inadequate substitute for the consummation that has failed to occur among the main characters. The alternative presented by the songs twits the anxiety it ostensibly seeks to mitigate by invoking the larger perspective of the natural cycle:

> The cuckoo then on every tree
> Mocks married men; for thus sings he,
>   "Cuckoo;
> Cuckoo, cuckoo"—O word of fear,
> Unpleasing to a married ear!
>   (5.2.898–902)

This apparently blithe epilogue mirrors the men's situation in the play proper by restating women's power to make or break men. It recapitulates but does not relieve the humiliation of men as helpless victims of female caprice.[3]

By contrast, *As You Like It* creates a context in which the efficaciousness of art is affirmed rather than denied.

The masque of Hymen anticipates the sanctified unity of a late romance by appealing to the trope of "wonder":

> Whiles a wedlock-hymn we sing,
> Feed yourselves with questioning;
> That reason wonder may diminish
> How thus we met, and these things finish.
>
> (5.4.137–40)

The equation of wedding with formal closure is indicated by Hymen's ostentatious use of words like "finish" and "conclusion": "Peace ho! I bar confusion, / 'Tis I must make conclusion" (125–26). This gratifying happy ending is convincing, however, because Hymen's role is not just a matter of external *deus ex machina*. In presenting Rosalind undisguised, the god of marriage claims that "Hymen from heaven brought her" (112), but we are entitled to feel that the reverse is true: Rosalind has brought Hymen. The character of Rosalind, the real coordinator of the final scene, stands behind the metaphor of magic she invokes for the play's resolution: "Believe then, if you please, that I can do strange things. I have, since I was three year old, convers'd with a magician, most profound in his art, and yet not damnable" (5.2.58–61). Rosalind has explored the limits of the magic that her male costume has afforded her in the forest of Arden. Like Prospero, she now gives up this magic, but she has earned her final throwaway use of it.

This comparative sketch of the endings of *Love's Labor's Lost* and *As You Like It* raises questions. How do we account for the difference between the two endings? How is the resolution of *As You Like It* achieved? A partial answer lies in Shakespeare's use of pastoral. In *Love's Labor's Lost*, pastoral applies only to the setting and general atmosphere but does not extend to the dramatic structure. The play sets up a contrast between two worlds: the court in which the men take refuge versus the field which the women insist on making their residence. However, the relationship between the two worlds is one of simple opposition. The static quality of this relationship leaves too little room for interplay between the worlds and leads directly to the stalemate of the conclusion. *As You Like It* dramatically expands the contrast and the possibilities for interaction between the two worlds of court and forest. The sharply differentiated landscapes unfold in sequence, making it possible for men to enter the green world and creating the dynamic three-part process identified by Barber and Northrop Frye.[4] This full realization of pastoral form in *As You Like It* gives Shakespeare an artistic leverage on his material that helps to make possible the final resolution.

While useful, this kind of structural comparison can take us only so far. Formal description is insufficient as a total explanation of the differences between *Love's Labor's Lost* and *As You Like It* because the respective uneasiness and confidence of their endings is a matter of the relations between men and women as well as of aesthetic form. Hence it becomes imperative to look at the plays from the perspective of sexual politics. From this perspective, Shakespeare's development from *Love's Labor's Lost* to *As You Like It* does not emerge as the unqualified advancement it might otherwise appear to be. The ending of *As You Like It* works smoothly because male control is affirmed and women are rendered nonthreatening whereas in *Love's Labor's Lost* women do not surrender their independence and the status of patriarchy remains in doubt. Harmony and disharmony have as much to do with the specific content of male–female relations as with aesthetic form.

In both *Love's Labor's Lost* and *As You Like It*, love brings out a disparity between male and female intelligence and power. Orlando, like the four lords, is transformed in a way that makes him look humorously but embarrassingly naïve and helpless. Falling in love is experienced as incapacitation:

> My better parts
> Are all thrown down, and that which here stands up
> Is but a quintain, a mere liveless block. . . .
> O poor Orlando! thou art overthrown
> Or Charles, or something weaker, masters thee.
>
> (1.2.249–51, 259–60)

His sense of being mastered helps to create a one-sided relationship in which the woman has control. Again like the four lords, Orlando equates being in love with the reflex gesture of producing huge quantities of poetry, and he follows a poetic convention that further increases the woman's power:

> Thus Rosalind of many parts
>   By heavenly synod was devis'd
> Of many faces, eyes, and hearts,
>   To have the touches dearest priz'd.
> Heaven would that she these gifts should have,
> And I to live and die her slave.
>
> (3.2.149–54)

The mechanical and impersonal nature of this elevation of the woman to divine status is demonstrated by the way Orlando's poem invents her through an amalgamation of fantasized "parts." Worship of the woman that is supposed to pay homage creates an inhuman pastiche that demeans her and inhibits genuine contact. Such obeisance also belittles the man since Orlando's poem defines a sharply hierarchical relationship in which his idealization of Rosalind as the perfect goddess leaves him with the role—exaggerated in the opposite direction—of "slave."[5] The servility implied by poetic worship is taken a step further in the case of Silvius, whose "holy" and "perfect" love make him content "To glean the broken ears after the man / That the main harvest reaps" (3.5.99, 102–3). Rosalind's observation that Orlando's verse is "lame" (3.2.168) refers not only to the poem's execution but also to the psychological stance Orlando adopts toward her.

Rosalind is thus placed in a position parallel to that of the ladies in *Love's Labor's Lost*. Like them, she is strong and manipulative as she uses her superior wit along with the advantages given to her by circumstance to disabuse Orlando of his stock notions of male and female roles in love. There is, however, a vast difference in the outcome of this process in the two plays because Rosalind proves to be more flexible and accommodating than the women of *Love's Labor's Lost*. Her response to Phebe and Silvius is an attack on sonnet convention that implicitly involves a self-education for Rosalind. In upbraiding the two for their enactment of the stereotype of female scorn and male abasement, she is as critical of Silvius (3.5.49–56) as of Phebe. Rosalind's effort to put Phebe in her place is accompanied by her attempt to bring Silvius up to his place. This double lesson has an application to her own behavior since Rosalind's decision to "speak to him like a saucy lackey, and under that habit to play the knave with him" (3.2.295–97) carries the danger that she will allow herself to be as "proud and pitiless" (3.5.40) as she accuses Phebe of being, while Orlando languishes in Silvius-like submissiveness. Observing this dynamic at work in another relation alerts her to the potential Phebe in herself. Rosalind thus proves a more "busy actor in their play" (3.4.59) than she had anticipated; her fervent effort to convince Phebe to adopt more tractable behavior becomes an argument that she must accept her own advice. Rosalind's capacity to give up this pride is what allows *As You Like It* to extricate itself from the poetic postures of male subservience and female omnipotence in which *Love's Labor's Lost* remains fixed to the bitter end.

If Rosalind's flexibility is the key reason that *As You Like It* ends "like an old play" with "Jack having his Gill," we must go on to ask: what is the nature of this flexibility? and is the absence of it in *Love's Labor's Lost* entirely in *As You Like It*'s favor? The standard approach stresses that Rosalind has a larger emotional range than the ladies of

Love's Labor's Lost. She is more impressive because more complex and more humane. The encounter between Rosalind and Jaques at the beginning of act 4, scene 1, makes clear her rejection of his detachment: "I fear you have sold your own lands to see other men's; then to have seen much, and to have nothing, is to have rich eyes and poor hands" (22–25). Her direct experience and involvement distinguish her from the women of *Love's Labor's Lost,* who in the end "have nothing." But a second approach sees Rosalind as a woman who submits to a man who is her inferior.[6] The power symbolized by her male costume is only temporary, and the harmonious conclusion is based on her willingness to relinquish this power. Thus Rosalind's passionate involvement has a significant negative side since involvement means co-option and assimilation by a society ruled by men. She escapes the female stereotype of the all-powerful woman created by lyrical inflation only at the price of succumbing to another stereotype: the compliant, essentially powerless woman fostered by practical patriarchal politics.

Before entering the forest of Arden, Rosalind's companion Celia/Aliena redefines this pastoral space to mean opportunity rather than punishment: "Now go we in content / To liberty, and not to banishment" (1.3.137–38). This "liberty" implies overcoming the restrictions of the female role. The idea of the male disguise originates as a strategy for avoiding the normal vulnerability to male force: "Alas, what danger will it be to us, / Maids as we are, to travel forth so far! / Beauty provoketh thieves sooner than gold" (108–10). Rosalind's male costume, as it evolves, expands her identity so that she can play both male and female roles. Yet the costume is problematic. Though it gives her freedom of action and empowers her to take the initiative with Orlando, it simultaneously serves as a protective device, which temptingly offers excessive security, even invulnerability. In order to love, Rosalind must reveal herself directly to Orlando, thereby making herself vulnerable. She must give up the disguise and appear—as she ultimately promises Orlando—"human as she is" (5.2.67). But in giving up the disguise, she also gives up the strength it symbolizes. As the disguise begins to break down before its official removal, Rosalind's transparent femininity takes the form of fainting—a sign of weakness that gives her away: "You a man? / You lack a man's heart" (4.3.163–64). This loss of control signals that Rosalind can no longer deny her inner feminine self. The capacity for love that we find so admirable in Rosalind is compromised by the necessity that she resume a traditional female role in order to engage in love.

This traditional image has been present all along. Rosalind willingly confides to Celia that she remains a woman despite the male costume: "in my heart / Lie there what hidden woman's fear there will— / We'll have a swashing and a martial outside" (1.3.118–20); "Good my complexion, dost thou think, though I am caparison'd like a man, I have a doublet and hose in my disposition?" (3.2.194–96); and "Do you not know I am a woman?" (249). By virtue of the costume, Rosalind does have access to both male and female attributes, but the impression she conveys of androgynous wholeness is misleading. Neither Rosalind nor the play questions the conventional categories of masculine and feminine. She does not reconcile gender definitions in the sense of integrating or synthesizing them. Her own insistence on the metaphor of exterior (male) and interior (female) keeps the categories distinct and separable. The liberation that Rosalind experiences in the forest has built into it the conservative countermovement by which, as the play returns to the normal world, she will be reduced to the traditional woman who is subservient to men.

Rosalind is shown working out in advance the terms of her return. Still protected by her disguise yet allowing herself to come closer to the decisive moment, she instructs Orlando to "woo me" (4.1.68) and subsequently tells him what to say in a wedding rehearsal while she practises yielding. Though she teases Orlando with the wife's power to make him a cuckold and then to conceal her duplicity with her "wayward wit" (160–76), this is good fun, and it is only that. It is clear to the audience, if not yet to Orlando, that Rosalind's flaunting of her role as disloyal wife is a put-on rather than a genuine threat. She may playfully delay the final moment when she becomes a wife, but we are reassured that, once married, she will in fact be faithful. Her humor has the effect of exorcising and renouncing her potential weapon. The uncertainty concerns not her loyalty but Orlando's, as her sudden change of tone when he announces his departure indicates: "Alas, dear love, I cannot lack thee two hours!" (178). Her exuberance and control collapse in fears of his betrayal: "Ay, go your ways, go your ways; I knew what you would prove" (182–83). Her previous wit notwithstanding, for Rosalind the scene is less a demonstration of power than an exercise in vulnerability. She is once again consigned to anxious waiting for her tardy man: "But why did he swear he would come this morning, and comes not?" (3.4.18–19).

Rosalind's own behavior neutralizes her jokes about cuckoldry, but this point is sharply reinforced by the brief account of the male hunt that immediately follows act 4, scene 1. The expected negative meaning of horns as the sign of a cuckold is transformed into a positive image of phallic potency that unites men. Changing the style of his literary response to deer killing, Jaques replaces his earlier lament (2.1.26–66) with a celebration of male hunt and conquest: "Let's present him to the Duke like a Roman conqueror, and it would do well to set the deer's horns upon his head, for a branch of victory" (4.2.3–5).[7] The rousing song occasioned by this moment suggests the power of an all-male activity to provide a self-sufficient male heritage, thus to defend against male insecurity about humiliation by women.

The final scene, orchestrated by Rosalind, demonstrates her power in a paradoxical way. She is the architect of a resolution that phases out the control she has wielded and prepares the way for the patriarchal status quo. She accedes to the process by which, in the transition from courtship to marriage, power passes from the female to the male: the man is no longer the suitor who serves, obeys, and begs but is now the husband who commands. Rosalind's submission is explicit but not ironic, though her tone may be high-spirited. To each of the two men in her life she declares: "To you I give myself, for I am yours" (5.4.116–17). Her casting herself in the role of male possession is all the more charming because she does not have to be forced to adopt it: her self-taming is voluntary. We may wish to give Rosalind credit for her cleverness in forestalling male rivalry between her father and her fiancé. Unlike Cordelia, she is smart enough to see that in order to be gratified, each man needs to feel that he is the recipient of all her love, not half of it. Yet Rosalind is not really in charge here because the potential hostility between the younger and older man has already been negotiated in the forest in act 2, scene 7, a negotiation that results in the formation of an idealized male alliance. Rosalind submits not only to two individual men but also to the patriarchal society that they embody. Patriarchy is not a slogan smuggled in from the twentieth century and imposed on the play but an exact term for the social structure that close reading reveals within the play.

II

We are apt to assume that the green world is more free than it actually is. In the case of *As You Like It*, the green world cannot be interpreted as a space apart where a youthful rebellion finds a refuge from the older generation. The forest of Arden includes a strong parental presence: Duke Senior's is the first voice we hear there. Moreover, the green world has a clear political structure. Freed from the constraints of courtly decorum, Duke Senior can afford to address his companions as "brothers" (2.1.1), but he nonetheless retains a fatherly command. Fraternal spirit is not equivalent to democracy, as is clarified when the duke dispenses favor on a hierarchical basis: "Shall share the good of our returned fortune, / According to the measure of their states" (5.4.174–75).

Although interpretations of *As You Like It* often stress youthful love, we should not neglect the paternal context in which the love occurs. Both Rosalind and Orlando acknowledge Duke Senior. Rosalind is aware, as she finds herself attracted to Orlando, that "My father lov'd Sir Rowland [Orlando's father] as his soul" (1.2.235) and hence that her affection is not incompatible with family approval. Orlando, for his part, does not go forward in pursuit of love until after he has become friends with Duke Senior. Rosalind and Orlando approach the forest in strikingly different ways. Rosalind's mission is love. Upon entering the forest, she discovers there the love "passion" she has brought with her: "Alas, poor shepherd, searching of thy wound, / I have by hard adventure found mine own" (2.4.44–45). Orlando, by contrast, has two projects (though he does not consciously formulate them) to complete in the forest: the first is his quest to reestablish the broken connection with his father's legacy; the second is the quest for Rosalind. The sequence of these projects is an indication of priority. Orlando's outburst—"But heavenly Rosalind!" (1.2.289)—is not picked up again until he opens act 3, scene 2, with his love poem. The interim is reserved for his other, patriarchal business.

In the first scene of the play, Orlando makes it clear, in a melodramatic but nonetheless poignant way, that he derives his sense of identity from his dead father, an identity that is not yet fulfilled. In protesting against his older brother's mistreatment, Orlando asserts the paternal bond: "The spirit of my father grows strong in me, and I will no longer endure it" (1.1.70–71). His first step toward recovery of the connection with his lost father is the demolition of Charles the wrestler: "How dost thou, Charles?" / "He cannot speak, my lord" (1.2.219–20). This victory earns Orlando the right to proclaim his father's name as his own:

DUKE F.   What is thy name, young man?
ORL.   Orlando, my liege, the youngest son of Sir Rowland de Boys. . . .
I am more proud to be Sir Rowland's son.

(221–22, 232)

Frederick's negative reaction to Orlando's statement of identity confirms the concept of heritage being evoked here: "Thou shouldst have better pleas'd me with this deed / Hadst thou descended from another house" (227–28). The significance of the wrestling match is that Orlando has undergone a traditional male rite of passage, providing an established channel for the violence he has previously expressed by collaring Oliver in the opening scene. Yet aggression is the epitome of a rigid masculinity that Shakespeare characteristically condemns as too narrow a basis for identity. Orlando's aggressiveness is instantly rendered inappropriate by his falling in love. Moreover, his recourse to violence simply mirrors the technique of the tyrannical Duke Frederick. As it turns out, Orlando must give up violence in order to meet the "good father."

While Rosalind's confidante Celia provides the opportunity to talk about love, Orlando is accompanied by Adam, who serves a very different function since he is a living link to Orlando's father. The paternal inheritance blocked by Oliver is received indirectly from Adam when he offers the money "I sav'd under your father, / Which I did store to be my foster-nurse" (2.3.39–40). The motif of nurturance implied by the "foster-nurse" image is continued as Orlando, through Adam's sudden collapse from lack of food, is led to Duke Senior's pastoral banquet. Treating this new situation as another trial of "the strength of my youth," Orlando imagines an all-or-nothing "adventure" (1.2.172,

177) similar to the wrestling match: "If this uncouth forest yield any thing savage, I will either be food for it, or bring it for food to thee" (2.6.6–8). In act 2, scene 7, he enters with drawn sword. Unexpectedly finding a benevolent father figure, Orlando effects as gracefully as possible a transition from toughness to tenderness: "Let gentleness my strong enforcement be, / In the which hope I blush, and hide my sword" (118–19). This display of nonviolence is the precondition for Orlando's recovery of patriarchal lineage. Duke Senior aids this recovery by his recognition of the father's reflection in the son and by his declaration of his own loving connection with Orlando's father. This transaction concludes the scene:

> If that you were the good Sir Rowland's son,
> As you have whisper'd faithfully you were,
> And as mine eye doth his effigies witness
> Most truly limn'd and living in your face,
> Be truly welcome hither. I am the Duke
> That lov'd your father.
>
> (191–96)

The confirmation of Orlando's identity has the effect of a ritual blessing that makes this particular father–son relation the basis for social cohesion in general. There is much virtue in Orlando's "If":

> ORL. If ever you have look'd on better days,
> If ever been where bells have knoll'd to church,
> If ever sate at any good man's feast,
> If ever from your eyelids wip'd a tear,
> And know what 'tis to pity, and be pitied. . . .
>
> DUKE S. True is it that we have seen better days,
> And have with holy bell been knoll'd to church,
> And sat at good men's feasts, and wip'd our eyes
> Of drops that sacred pity hath engend'red.
>
> (2.7.113–17, 120–23)

The liturgy of male utopia, ruthlessly undercut in *Love's Labor's Lost*, is here allowed to stand. Virgilian piety, founded on ideal father–son relations and evoked visually when, like Aeneas with Anchises, Orlando carries Adam on his back, can achieve what Navarre's academe with its spurious abstinence could not. Orlando's heroic language as he goes off to rescue Adam is as clumsy as any he uses in the poems to Rosalind, but whereas the play pokes fun at the love poetry, the expression of duty to Adam is not subject to irony: "Then but forbear your food a little while, / Whiles, like a doe, I go to find my fawn, / And give it food" (127–29). We are invited simply to accept the doe-fawn metaphor that Orlando invokes for his obligation to reciprocate Adam's "pure love" (131).

Just as there is an unlimited supply of food in this scene, so there seems to be more than enough "pure love" to go around, Jaques excepted. Love is expressed in terms of food, and men gladly take on nurturant roles. Duke Senior's abundant provision of food and of "gentleness" creates an image of a self-sustaining patriarchial system. The men take over the traditional female prerogative of maternal nurturance, negatively defined by Jaques: "At first the infant, / Mewling and puking in the nurse's arms" (2.7.143–44). Such discomfort has been purged from the men's nurturance as it is dramatized in this scene, which thus offers a new perspective on Duke Senior's very first speech in the play. We now see that it is the male feast, not the biting winter wind, that "feelingly persuades me what I am" (2.1.11). "Sweet are the uses of adversity" because, as Orlando discovers, adversity disappears when men's "gentleness" prevails, "translating the stubbornness of fortune / Into so quiet and sweet a style" (12, 19–20). This sweetness explains why "loving lords have put themselves into voluntary exile" with the duke and why "many young gentlemen flock to him every day" (1.1.101–2, 117).

The idealized male enclave founded on "sacred pity" in act 2, scene 7, is not an isolated incident. The power of male pity extends beyond this scene to include the evil Oliver, who is threatened by a symbol of maternal nurturance made hostile by depletion: "A lioness, with udders all drawn dry" (4.3.114) and "the suck'd and hungry lioness" (126). The motif of eating here creates a negative image that might disturb the comfortable pastoral banquet, but the lioness's intrusion is quickly ended. Responding with a kindness that can be traced back to his meeting with Duke Senior, Orlando rescues his brother: "But kindness, nobler ever than revenge, / And nature, stronger than his just occasion, / Made him give battle to the lioness" (128–30). Oliver's oral fulfillment follows: "my conversion / So sweetly tastes" (136–37). The tears "that sacred pity hath engend'red" (2.7.123) are reiterated by the brothers' reconciliation—"Tears our recountments had most kindly bath'd" (4.3.140)—and their reunion confirmed by a recapitulation of the banquet scene: "he led me to the gentle Duke, / Who gave me fresh array and entertainment, / Committing me unto my brother's love" (142–44). Again the pattern of male reconciliation preceding love for women is seen in Oliver's confession of his desire to marry Celia (5.2.1–14) coming after his admission to the brotherhood.

The male community of act 2, scene 7, is also vindicated by the restoration of patriarchal normalcy in the play's final scene. In the end, as Rosalind's powers are fading, the relationship between Duke Senior and Orlando is reasserted and completed as the duke announces the inheritance to which marriage entitles Orlando: "A land itself at large, a potent dukedom" (5.4.169). Like the "huswife Fortune" who "doth most mistake in her gifts to women" (1.2.31–32, 36), Rosalind plays her part by rehearsing the men in their political roles:

ROS.   You say, if I bring in your Rosalind,
            You will bestow her on Orlando here?
DUKE S. That would I, had I kingdoms to give with her.
ROS.   And you say you will have her, when I bring her.
ORL.   That would I, were I of all kingdoms king.

                                       (5.4.6–10)

The reference the two men make to kingdoms is shortly to be fulfilled, but this bounty is beyond Rosalind's power to give. For it is not her magic that produces the surprise entrance of Jaques de Boys with the news of Duke Senior's restoration. In completing the de Boys family reunion, the middle brother's appearance reverses the emblematic fate of the three sons destroyed by Charles the wrestler: "Yonder they lie, the poor old man, their father, making such pitiful dole over them that all the beholders take his part with weeping" (1.2.129–32). The image of three de Boys sons reestablishes the proper generational sequence, ensuring continuity.

III

C. L. Barber has shown that the "Saturnalian Pattern" that gives structure to festive comedy is intrinsically conservative since it involves only "a temporary license, a 'misrule' which implied rule."[8] But in *As You Like It* the conservatism of comic form does not affect all characters equally. In the liberal opening out into the forest of Arden, both men and women are permitted an expansion of sexual identity that transcends restrictive gender roles. Just as Rosalind gains access to the traditional masculine attributes of strength and control through her costume, so Orlando gains access to the traditional female attributes of compassion and nurturance. However, the conservative countermovement built into comic strategy applies exclusively to Rosalind. Her possession of the male costume and of the power it symbolizes is only temporary. But Orlando does not have to give up the emotional enlargement he has experienced in the forest. Discussions of androgyny in *As You Like It* usually focus on Rosalind whereas in fact it is the men rather than the women who are the lasting beneficiaries of androgyny. It is Orlando, not Rosalind, who achieves a synthesis of attributes traditionally labeled masculine and feminine when he combines compassion and aggression in rescuing his brother from the lioness.

This selective androgyny demands an ambivalent response: it is a humanizing force for the men, yet it is based on the assumption that men have power over women.[9] Because androgyny is available only to men, we are left with a paradoxical compatibility of androgyny with patriarchy, that is, benevolent patriarchy. In talking about male power in *As You Like It*, we must distinguish between two forms of patriarchy. The first and most obvious is the harsh, mean-spirited version represented by Oliver, who abuses primogeniture, and by Duke Frederick, who after usurping power holds on to it by arbitrary acts of suppression. Driven by greed, envy, suspicion, and power for power's sake, neither man can explain his actions. In an ironic demonstration of the consuming nature of evil, Duke Frederick expends his final rage against Oliver, who honestly protests: "I never lov'd my brother in my life" (3.1.14). In contrast to good men, bad men are incapable of forming alliances. Since Frederick's acts of banishment have now depopulated the court, he himself must enter the forest in order to seek the enemies so necessary to his existence (5.4.154–58). But of course this patriarchal tyranny is a caricature and therefore harmless. Oliver and Frederick are exaggerated fairy-tale villains whose hardened characters are unable to withstand the wholesome atmosphere of the forest and instantly dissolve (4.3.135–37; 5.4.159–65). The second, more serious version of patriarchy is the political structure headed by Duke Senior. To describe it, we seek adjectives like "benevolent," "humane," and "civilized." Yet we cannot leave it at that. A benevolent patriarchy still requires women to be subordinate, and Rosalind's final performance is her enactment of this subordination.

We can now summarize the difference between the conclusions of *Love's Labor's Lost* and *As You Like It*. In order to assess the sense of an ending, we must take into account the perspective of sexual politics and correlate formal harmony or disharmony with patriarchal stability or instability. Unlike Rosalind, the women in *Love's Labor's Lost* do not give up their independence.[10] The sudden announcement of the death of the princess's father partially restrains her wit. But this news is a *pater ex machina* attempt to even the score and to equalize the situation between the men and the women because nothing has emerged organically within the play to challenge the women's predominance. The revelation that the "decrepit, sick and bedred" father (1.1.138) has died is not an effective assertion of his presence but, on the contrary, advertises his weakness. The princess submits to the "new-sad soul" (5.2.731) that mourning requires, but this provides the excuse for going on to reject the suitors as she has all along. Her essential power remains intact, whereas patriarchal authority is presented as weak or nonexistent. The death of the invalid father has a sobering impact because it mirrors the vacuum created by the four lords' powerlessness within the play. There is no relief from the fear that dominant women inspire in a patriarchal sensibility, and this continuing tension contributes to the uneasiness at the play's end.

Like the princess, Rosalind confronts her father in the final scene. But in her case paternal power is vigorously represented by Duke Senior and by the line of patriarchal authority established when Senior makes Orlando his heir. Festive celebration is now possible because a dependable, that is, patriarchal, social order is securely in place. It is Duke Senior's voice that legitimates the festive closure: "Play, music, and you brides and bridegrooms all, / With measure heap'd in joy, to th' measures fall" (5.4.178–79). Orlando benefits from this social structure because, in contrast to the lords of *Love's Labor's Lost*, he has a solid political resource to offset the liability of a poetic convention that dictates male subservience. *As You Like It* achieves marital closure not by eliminating male ties but rather by strengthening them.[11]

A further phasing out of Rosalind occurs in the Epilogue when it is revealed that she is male: "If I were a woman I would kiss as many of you as had beards that pleas'd me" (18–19). This explicit breaking of theatrical illusion forces us to reckon with the fact of an all-male cast. The boy-actor convention makes it possible for males to explore the female other (I use the term *other* here in the sense given by Simone de Beauvoir in *The Second Sex* of woman as the other). Vicariously taking on the female role enables male spectators to make an experimental contact with what otherwise might remain unknown, forbidden territory. Fear of women can be encountered in the relatively safe environment of the theater, acted out, controlled (when it can be controlled as in *As You Like It*), and overcome. A further twist of logic defuses and reduces the threat of female power: Rosalind is no one to be frightened of since, as the Epilogue insists, she is male after all; she is only a boy and clearly subordinate to men in the hierarchy of things.

The convention of males playing female roles gives men the opportunity to imagine sex-role fluidity and flexibility. Built into the conditions of performance is the potential for male acknowledgment of a "feminine self" and thus for male transcendence of a narrow masculinity. In the particular case of *As You Like It,* the all-male cast provides a theatrical counterpart for the male community at Duke Senior's banquet in act 2, scene 7. This theatrical dimension reinforces the conservative effect of male androgyny within the play. Acknowledgment of the feminine within the male is one thing, the acknowledgment of individual women another: the latter does not automatically follow from the former. In the boy-actor motif, woman is a metaphor for the male discovery of the feminine within himself, of those qualities suppressed by a masculinity strictly defined as aggressiveness. Once the tenor of the metaphor has been attained, the vehicle can be discarded—just as Rosalind is discarded. The sense of the patriarchal ending in *As You Like It* is that male androgyny is affirmed whereas female "liberty" in the person of Rosalind is curtailed.

There is, finally, a studied ambiguity about heterosexual versus homoerotic feeling in the play, Shakespeare allowing himself to have it both ways. The Epilogue is heterosexual in its bringing together of men and women: "and I charge you, O men, for the love you bear to women (as I perceive by your simp'ring, none of you hates them), that between you and the women the play may please" (14–17). The "simp'ring" attributed to men in their response to women is evoked in a good-natured jocular spirit; yet the tone conveys discomfort as well. In revealing the self-sufficient male acting company, the Epilogue also offers the counterimage of male bonds based on the exclusion of women.

Though he is shown hanging love poems on trees only after achieving atonement with Rosalind's father, Orlando never tries, like the lords of *Love's Labor's Lost,* to avoid women. The social structure of *As You Like It,* in which political power is vested in male bonds, can include heterosexual love because marriage becomes a way of incorporating women since Rosalind is complicit in her assimilation by patriarchal institutions. However, in spite of the disarming of Rosalind, resistance to women remains. It is as though asserting the priority of relations between men over relations between men and women is not enough, as though a fall-back position is needed. The Epilogue is, in effect, a second ending that provides further security against women by preserving on stage the image of male ties in their pure form with women absent. Not only are women to be subordinate; they can, if necessary, be imagined as nonexistent. Rosalind's art does not, as is sometimes suggested, coincide with Shakespeare's: Shakespeare uses his art to take away Rosalind's female identity and thereby upstages her claim to magic power.

We can see the privileged status accorded to male bonds by comparing Shakespeare's treatment of same-sex relations for men and for women. Men originally divided are reunited as in the instance of Oliver and Orlando, but women undergo the reverse process. Rosalind and Celia are initially inseparable: "never two ladies lov'd as they do" (1.1.112); "whose loves / Are dearer than the natural bond of sisters" (1.2.275–76); "And whereso'er we went, like Juno's swans, / Still we went coupled and inseparable" (1.3.75–76); and "thou and I am one. / Shall we be sund'red? shall we part, sweet girl? / No, let my father seek another heir" (97–99). Yet the effect of the play is to separate them by transferring their allegiance to husbands. Celia ceases to be a speaking character at the end of act 4, her silence coinciding with her new role as fiancée. The danger of female bonding is illustrated when Shakespeare diminishes Rosalind's absolute control by mischievously confronting her with the unanticipated embarrassment of Phebe's love for her. Rosalind is of course allowed to devise an escape from the pressure of this undesirable entanglement, but it is made clear in the process that such ardor is taboo and that the authorized defense against it is marriage. "And so am I for no woman," Rosalind insists (5.2.88). A comparable prohibition is not announced against male friendship.[12]

In conclusion, we must ask: what is Shakespeare's relation to the sexual politics of *As You Like It?* Is he taking an ironic and critical stance toward the patriarchal solution of his characters, or is he heavily invested in this solution himself? I think there are limits to Shakespeare's critical awareness in this play. The sudden conversions of Oliver and Duke Frederick have a fairy-tale quality that Shakespeare clearly intends as an aspect of the wish fulfillment to which he calls attention in the play's title. Similarly, Jaques's commentary in the final scene is a deliberate foil to the neatness of the ending that allows Shakespeare as well as Jaques a modicum of distance. However, in fundamental respects Shakespeare appears to be implicated in the fantasy he has created for his characters.

As You Like It enacts two rites of which Shakespeare did not avail himself in *Love's Labor's Lost*. First, Shakespeare has the social structure ultimately contain female energy as he did not in *Love's Labor's Lost*. We have too easily accepted the formulation that says that Shakespeare in the mature history plays concentrates on masculine development whereas in the mature festive comedies he gives women their due by allowing them to play the central role.[13] *As You Like It* is primarily a defensive action against female power rather than a celebration of it. Second, Shakespeare portrays an ideal male community based on "sacred pity." This idealized vision of relationships between men can be seen as sentimental and unrealistic, but in contrast to his undercutting of academe in *Love's Labor's Lost*, Shakespeare is here thoroughly engaged and endorses the idealization. These two elements—female vitality kept manageable and male power kept loving—provided a resolution that at this particular moment was "As Shakespeare Liked It."

This chapter began with the suggestion that *Henry V* and *As You Like It* have in common a concern with father–son ties. The two plays are also connected by their treatment of mothers. Both plays deal with the problem of the mother simply by excluding it. The Henry IV–Henry V relationship occurs in a maternal vacuum; the absent mother enables Henry V to become "the motherless man."[14] Management of female vitality in *As You Like It* includes specific avoidance of women as mothers.[15] In Northrop Frye's view: "There is something maternal about the green world, in which the new order of the comic resolution is nourished and brought to birth."[16] But there is no effective maternal presence in *As You Like It*. The maternal force is confined to the emblematic angry lioness and summarily disposed of, thereby allowing the action of the play to unfold in an environment kept free of maternal interference. Rosalind contributes to this effect because she lacks sexual maturity: she is a prematernal and hence nonmaternal figure. Her transvestism hinges on the merging of "boys and women" (3.2.414) in the preadolescent moment prior to sharp gender differentiation. The occasional allusions to becoming pregnant (1.3.11; 3.2.204; 4.1.175) are only witty anticipations that have no immediate impact. The future in which the imagined pregnancy might become a reality is sufficiently distanced for us to feel that it is firmly held outside the bounds of the play. This defense against encroachment by the maternal through virtual exclusion of it serves to link *As You Like It* with *Henry V*.

2

Fathers, Sons,
and Brothers in *Henry V*

The problem many readers face in relation to *Henry V* is "what to make of a diminished thing." One group praises it while another faults it for being a one-dimensional epic pageant; but both groups share the assumption that the complexity of the *Henry IV* plays is drastically reduced or altogether eliminated in *Henry V*.[1] I reject this assumption and argue that in this final play of the second tetralogy, the locus of complexity has shifted. It no longer resides in the interrelationships among the four major characters— Henry IV, Falstaff, Hotspur, and Hal—but is now relocated within the dominant central consciousness of the single remaining character—Henry V—who has in effect absorbed the other three. This absorption ensures the continuing resonance of the missing figures. Henry IV functions as a source of stress and tension in the new king's language in *Henry V*. Henry V's identity is defined in relation to his father and his father's projects—a connection that makes the son vulnerable as well as powerful. Henry V lacks a separate, independent self whose voice can be clearly identified and trusted as his own. The self at cross-purposes is registered in the cross-currents in Henry V's language, which is far more interesting and haunting than has been acknowledged.[2]

One of the chief obstacles to a fresh, full reading of *Henry V* is the formulation of a sharp opposition between Henry V's public role and his private voice, concluding that the latter has vanished. The notion that Henry V is so totally consumed by his role as king that the man is squeezed out is a simplified and inaccurate way to speak about the intricacies of his character; it does not ring true to the intensity of his language and imagery or to our intimacy with him. The idiosyncratic personal voice may be constrained and turbid, but it is still unmistakably there. Henry V's speeches cannot be read (or heard in the theater) exclusively as public oration because this approach ignores or underestimates the involuted quality of his rhetoric. His speeches have an effect of soliloquy. They are technically addressed to others, but only the cinema—distorting text and theatrical conditions—can create a completely convincing illusion of a public setting. Because of their sheer length, the speeches turn inward and gain a life of their own partly detached from the particular external circumstance. The emotionally involved linguistic structures in which the king embroils himself convey a feeling of isolation that makes them reverberate with self-doubt and self-questioning. The king's remark to Erpingham—"I and my bosom must debate a while" (4.1.31)—applies more generally to all his long speeches.

The momentary outburst in the soliloquy on ceremony in act 4, scene 1, is not an exception because the inner pressures on Henry V's public rhetoric have been building up gradually and continuously to that breaking point. For example, in act 2, scene 2, the king sets a trap to expose the three traitors, but the rhetorical overkill of his excessively lengthy peroration (79–144) communicates self-exposure. His calculated description of the traitors as Actaeons begins to sound reflexive: "For your own reasons turn into your bosoms, / As dogs upon their masters, worrying you" (82–83). The king's language typically suggests this "worrying" effect, as though he is overdoing it, is trying too hard, and is on the verge of losing control. We are often left with the impression that Henry V is not entirely convinced of the role his own rhetoric strains to enact. The apparent inauthenticity in his eloquence communicates not the emptiness of a hollow man but rather the fullness of Henry V's distress and anguish. We are made to feel the presence (not simply the absence) of the "naked frailties" that underlie his "manly readiness."[3]

I

Before considering the vestige of Henry IV in *Henry V*, let us first trace the interdependence of father and son through the second tetralogy. In *Richard II*, Bolingbroke's first act as Henry IV is anxiously to call for his son. Lacking Richard II's multiplicity of inner selves, Henry IV uses Hal as an extension of himself on which to project incipient guilt about the deposition: "Can no man tell me of my unthrifty son? / 'Tis full three months since I did see him last. / If any plague hang over us, 'tis he" (5.3.1–3). In the first face-to-face meeting between Henry IV and Hal in *1 Henry IV*, father and son act as each other's conscience. The king begins by accusing Hal of being "the hot vengeance, and the rod of heaven, / To punish my mistreadings" (3.2.10–11) and then criticizes him for his failure to repeat the king's own success story. From the perspective of the audience, the irony lies in how much Hal is already his father's son. We have overheard Hal conceive a rise to power predicated on tactical calculations similar to his father's. Both men use festive ritual as a metaphor for creating a strategic impression. "But when they [holidays] seldom come, they wish'd for come, / And nothing pleaseth but rare accidents" (1.2.206–7) has its counterpart in "and so my state, / Seldom but sumptuous, show'd like a feast / And wan by rareness such solemnity" (3.2.57–59).

In taking on the role of his father in the "play extempore," Hal had labeled Falstaff "that father ruffian" (2.4.454) and clearly foreshadowed the eventual banishment: "I do, I will" (481). Given this clarity, how can we account for the difficulties in the relationship between

Henry IV and Hal? Neither father nor son can securely know exactly who the other is because of his theatrical sense of himself. Each sees himself through the eyes of the spectators and thinks in terms of staging maximum visual impact. Just as Hal envisions himself as a sun "breaking through the foul and ugly mists" (1.2.202), so his father describes himself as a comet and as "sunlike majesty / When it shines seldom in admiring eyes" (3.2.47, 79–80). Henry IV also uses clothing imagery to explain his self-presentation: "And dress'd myself in such humility," "Thus did I keep my person fresh and new, / My presence, like a robe pontifical, / Ne'er seen but wond'red at" (51, 55–57). This manipulation of public appearance, which proves politically successful for both father and son, constitutes a barrier in their relationship with each other. Yet at the same time the intense desire to remove all artifice is manifested when Hal reiterates his allegiance to his father:

> I will redeem all this on Percy's head
> And in the closing of some glorious day
> Be bold to tell you that I am your son,
> When I will wear a garment all of blood,
> And stain my favors in a bloody mask,
> Which wash'd away shall scour my shame with it.
>
> (132–37)

The possibility that "garment" and "mask" can be "wash'd away" suggests the longing to restore purity both to divine kingship and to the personal relationship between father and son.

The parallel meeting in *2 Henry IV* has the same agenda of dealing with guilt and follows the same cyclical pattern of paternal recrimination, filial submission, and final atonement. In both *1 Henry IV* and *2 Henry IV*, Henry IV opens with a sarcastic, self-pitying castigation of his son, which is followed by the son's promise to live up to his father's highest expectations, followed by swift reconciliation, followed by the dispatch of business. In view of

Warwick's confidence that "The Prince will in the perfectness of time / Cast off his followers" (2H4, 4.4.74–75), the lengthy negotiation between father and son may seem unnecessary. Yet while Warwick's attitude serves to underscore Henry IV's lack of perception, Warwick's perspective is in turn limiting. His clear-cut sense of Hal's obvious dedication is of little help in understanding Shakespeare's remarkably inclusive idea of politics. The myth that Henry IV and Henry V are consummate politicians who have no time or taste for feelings is belied by the way private emotions are insisted upon as part of the intimate transmission of political power. Warwick's reasonable account is inadequate because Henry IV must talk to Hal in person; Hal is the only person who can complete the transaction.

It is extraordinary how, even at the moment when loyalty is being declared, the image of parricide stands forth so vividly:

> Thus, my most royal liege,
> Accusing it, I put it on my head,
> To try with it, as with an enemy
> That had before my face murdered my father,
> The quarrel of a true inheritor.
> (4.5.164–68)

The crown becomes a third person through whose medium father and son can exchange and deflect violent anger while at the same time they are reconciled with each other. Henry IV summarizes his delight at the argument's outcome: "God put it in thy mind to take it hence, / That thou mightst win the more thy father's love, / Pleading so wisely in excuse of it!" (178–80). The particular phrasing of "win," "pleading," and "excuse" suggests a Lear-like demand that Hal's protests of devotion successfully gratify and placate.

It soon becomes clear that Henry IV's anger with Hal was a preliminary manifestation of his own guilt about the deposing of Richard II. Having elicited Hal's support, Henry IV is now able to relieve this sense of guilt directly by confiding it. The paradox of atonement is that Hal has gained his father's blessing instead of his initial curse, but the blessing itself is burdened, through the father's confession, with the potential curse of a tainted crown. It is within this crux that we can experience the peculiar nature of Hal's identification with his father. Hal as Henry V will not be an exact replica of Henry IV; rather, he becomes the father in the special sense of trying to be better than the father. This striving for improvement entails acceptance of the father since purification is Henry IV's express wish for his son. The permission is also an injunction. Henry V must surpass his father because that is the prearranged means of atoning with and for him.

In the standard psychoanalytic formulation developed by Ernst Kris in "Prince Hal's Conflict" (1948), Kris describes "the formulation of the superego":

> The Prince, in his thoughts, compares the King, his father, with an ideal of royal dignity far superior to the father himself. This ideal, derived from paternal figures but exalted and heightened, is his protection in the struggle against his parricidal impulses and against submission to the King.[4]

However, Hal-Henry V does not succeed in avoiding "submission to the King." The "ideal of royal dignity far superior to the father himself" is Henry IV's directive to his son at the moment of atonement. Hal does not simply use "his ideal of moral integrity as a reproachful contrast against his father"[5] since their reunion is based on sharing this ideal. The reconciliation made possible by Hal's expressions of duty and love is also a burden: "Aeneas *patrem umeris portans,* carrying one's father on one's back; a super-ego, which is also a historical destiny."[6] Along with the ideals of redemption and integrity, a sense of sin is inherited through Henry IV's acknowledgment of the impurities in his accession to the kingship. The pragmatic advice about how "to busy giddy minds / With foreign quarrels" (*2H4*, 4.5.213–14) tacitly concedes doubt about whether his "death / Changes the mood" (198–99). Thus, the atonement consists of both the insistence on purging evil and the original evil. This dual genesis of purification and guilt—in relation to the father—may be understood as the fashioning of Henry V's reformation conscience.

Henry V's first speech after his father's death moves back and forth between acknowledging the appropriateness of mourning and arguing against the need for it. Surprisingly, the primary message is Henry V's gaiety. The traditional paradox—Le roi est mort; vive le roi!—has a special twist here because of the father–son identification that Henry V's exhilaration conveys in the punning on Harry: "Yet weep that Harry's dead, and so will I, / But Harry lives, that shall convert those tears / By number into hours of happiness" (5.2.59–61). As "the person of your father" and "the image of his power" (73–74), the Lord Chief Justice symbolizes the survival of the dead king and serves as the means by which Hal's private submission to his father can be translated into an institutional norm. The renewal of Henry IV in Henry V's kingship is implied by casting the Lord Chief Justice in a paternal posture, which is then internalized: "You shall be as a father to my youth, / My voice shall sound as you do prompt mine ear" (118–19). The extent of Henry V's incorporation of his father is most forcefully stated by direct invocation: "My father is gone wild into his grave, / For in his tomb lie my affections, / And with his spirits sadly I survive" (123–25). The earlier stress on "happiness" (61) is now disrupted by a more somber implication. Father and son are so intertwined that their sacrifice is mutual; we cannot say that the father, as scapegoat, carries off the son's "affections" (124) without also noting that the son "sadly" carries on his father's "spirits" (125).

Emphasis on Hal's choice of loyalty to his father over subversive alliance with Falstaff is not, however, the most fruitful way to see the *Henriad*. A sense of guilt informs both the atonement with Henry IV and the banishment of Falstaff, and the simultaneous occurrence of these two events at the close of 2 *Henry IV* should be treated as a single comprehensive gesture. Total embrace and total rejection are united as the two extreme, polar actions available to Hal-Henry V's guilt-ridden conscience. This sense of guilt underlies the epic surface of *Henry V*. We are faced in the final play of the second tetralogy with the paradox that although neither Falstaff nor Henry IV is actually present, both their presences are felt nonetheless. Both are scapegoats who refuse to stay away. Allusions to Falstaff and to Henry IV are trouble spots that make us feel uncomfortable about the official military victory, though they certainly do not prevent it. The net effect is to reopen the issues that Henry V had appeared to have conclusively resolved at the end of 2 *Henry IV*.

Falstaff's absence in *Henry V* is made obtrusive by Quickly's narration of his death in act 2, scene 3. His banishment is amusingly but awkwardly recalled in the midst of the battle of Agincourt by Fluellen's methodical Plutarchan parallel. When Fluellen says of "the fat knight with the great belly doublet"—"I have forgot his name" (4.7.48–50), we can readily supply the answer. Like Henry IV, Falstaff retains the ghostlike capacity to resurrect himself at a critical moment. Despite his insistence on the differences between Alexander the Pig and Harry of Monmouth, Fluellen's mispronunciation and his thesauruslike dwelling on Alexander's "rages, and his furies, and his wraths, and his cholers, and his moods, and his displeasures, and his indignations" (34–36) produce comic embarrassment rather than comic relief. Finally, we are reminded of Falstaff through the lesser remaining versions of him in the progeny consisting of Pistol, Bardolph, and Nym, all of whom receive banishmentlike treatment.

Henry IV is evoked at the outset of *Henry V* by Canterbury's rhapsodic marveling over the way the new king's purity commenced with his father's death:

> The breath no sooner left his father's body,
> But that his wildness, mortified in him,
> Seem'd to die too; yea, at that very moment,
> Consideration like an angel came
> And whipt th' offending Adam out of him,
> Leaving his body as a paradise
> T' envelop and contain celestial spirits.
> Never was such a sudden scholar made;
> Never came reformation in a flood
> With such a heady currance, scouring faults;
> Nor never Hydra-headed willfulness
> So soon did lose his seat (and all at once)
> As in this king.
>
> (1.1.25–37)

Henry V's own account in 2 *Henry IV* (5.2.123–29) is explicitly carried into the new play and embellished by Canterbury's review. The crescendo of triple "nevers" that round off his speech draws our attention to the embellishment. This hyperbolic image of Henry V's perfect soul is sometimes taken as an achieved reality, but the archbishop's prominently placed speech names the play's agenda only in the sense that it announces a theme to be probed dramatically. The king as an actual character, though sensitive to matters of conscience, never assumes the paradisal poise with the ease Canterbury suggests here. Ultimately, Henry V is deprived of this pleasant angelic image when, before Agincourt, he is forced to face the negative side of his relationship with his father. But even Canterbury cannot believe in the miracle wrought by his own rhetoric: "for miracles are ceas'd; / And therefore we must needs admit the means / How things are perfected" (1.1.67–69). If Hal's "veil of wildness" (64) is a strategy belonging to "the art and practic part of life" (51), so may be his spectacular "reformation" (33). Somewhere between the masks of wildness and of angelic consideration may lie the truth of Henry V's identity, which cannot be uttered in the "sweet and honeyed sentences" "men's ears" (50, 49) are so ready to consume.

The drama of the new king's identity is presented as a tension between two versions of paternal inheritance. The first is a heroic call that sidesteps the guilt associated with Henry IV and recovers an earlier father, Edward III. Canterbury absolves the king's conscience by shifting from a religious to a military vision:

> Stand for your own, unwind your bloody flag,
> Look back into your mighty ancestors;
> Go, my dread lord, to your great-grandsire's tomb,
> From whom you claim; invoke his warlike spirit,
> And your great-uncle's, Edward the Black Prince,
> Who on the French ground play'd a tragedy,
> Making defeat on the full power of France,
> Whiles his most mighty father on a hill
> Stood smiling to behold his lion's whelp
> Forage in blood of French nobility.
>
> (1.2.101–10)

If Henry V can perform the role of son by duplicating the Black Prince's feat, he can win the unqualified approval of the watchful, powerful father. As the play metaphor attests, this prospect involves the calculated construction of an identity, one offering physical danger but relative psychological safety. The son will "play a tragedy" at which the father will "smile"; this model of father–son relations produces a style of conscience so immune (or so impervious) that it mixes genres with impunity, freely converting aggression into pleasure.

The appeal of Edward III and of the Black Prince is kept before us by subsequent references. The French king echoes Canterbury's account (2.4.50–64); Henry V's claim points to "this most memorable line" (2.4.88), a "pedigree" proving him "evenly deriv'd / From his most fam'd of famous ancestors, / Edward the Third" (90–93); finally,

Fluellen dutifully echoes the chronicle sources (4.7.92–95). Yet Henry V is unable simply to fulfill the destiny promised to him as a "heroical seed" (2.4.59) because he cannot completely disregard the more problematic alternative: the image, closer to home, of his own father. Initially, the play skirts this difficulty, glancing at "the scambling and unquiet time" during "the last king's reign" (1.1.4, 2). Henry V preserves the ideal of a purified and unified England by ordering the death of the conspirator who falsely remarked: "those that were your father's enemies / Have steep'd their galls in honey, and do serve you / With hearts create of duty and of zeal" (2.2.29–31). But prior to the climactic battle at Agincourt, the king trips on his own logic and stumbles into a painful confrontation with the lingering issue of his father's guilty conscience.

Pressed to defend his "cause" (4.1.127) to the common soldiers while in the "shape" of "a common man" (4.8.53, 50), Henry V resorts to the metaphor of father and son: "So, if a son that is by his father sent about merchandise do sinfully miscarry upon the sea, the imputation of his wickedness, by your rule, should be impos'd upon his father that sent him. . . . But this is not so" (4.1.147–55). His argument, in keeping the sins of the son from being visited on the father, strictly separates their destinies. In the soliloquy soon to follow, when he protects himself from his father's sins, Henry V tries to insist on the same absolute separation. He attempts to admit his father's "fault" while simultaneously suspending it so that he cannot be contaminated: "Not to-day, O Lord, / O, not to-day, think not upon the fault / My father made in compassing the crown!" (292–94). The weakness of this effort is indicated by the plea to "think not upon"—purity can now be achieved only by consciously ignoring the impurities of which Henry V is in fact acutely aware.

In soliloquy, Henry V pursues his original purpose—"I and my bosom must debate a while" (4.1.31)—with a seriousness he had not intended. However effectively he comports himself when placed on the spot by the common soldiers, the king is riled by their challenge. In debate with his men, he deflects attention away from his own responsibility by insisting on theirs: "Every subject's duty is the King's, but every subject's soul is his own. Therefore should every soldier in the wars do as every sick man in his bed, wash every mote out of his conscience" (176–80). Thrown back on himself in soliloquy, Henry V sharply reverses himself, taking on the sin he has been at pains to keep at bay:

> Upon the King! let us our lives, our souls,
> Our debts, our careful wives,
> Our children, and our sins lay on the King!
> We must bear all.
>
> (230–33)

The king portrays himself as a scapegoat only sarcastically, out of frustration. The sins are still his subjects', not his. Yet Henry V's attack on the symbols of the regal power he has inherited suggests a more personal grappling with his own conscience.

The second part of his soliloquy is more specific in naming the source of sin:[7]

> I Richard's body have interred new,
> And on it have bestowed more contrite tears,
> Than from it issued forced drops of blood.
> Five hundred poor I have in yearly pay,
> Who twice a day their wither'd hands hold up
> Toward heaven, to pardon blood; and I have built
> Two chauntries, where the sad and solemn priests
> Sing still for Richard's soul. More will I do;
> Though all that I can do is nothing worth,
> Since that my penitence comes after all,
> Imploring pardon.
>
> (4.1.295–305)

Henry V's generalized railing against the helplessness of "idol Ceremony" (240) is now given concrete meaning by this enumeration of ritual activities for Richard II. The mechanical and quantitative nature of the ceremony, Henry V's flat, weary tone in reviewing it, and his direct confession of failure—"all that I can do is nothing worth"—indicate the hopelessness of his attempt at expiation. Nevertheless, he tries to contain the eruption of guilt by labeling it his father's problem: it is "the fault / My father made" rather than his own fault. Henry V's genuinely "contrite tears" (296) are futile "since that my penitence comes after all" (304), that is, after his father's deed. But the very process of protecting Henry V's purity by confining the blame to Henry IV suggests its implausibility. Because of the indissoluble union of father and son that derives from their original atonement, Henry V cannot so easily scapegoat his father. The sense of resignation the new king conveys in this moment is an oblique admission that his own royal power as well as his father's may be contaminated. Yet Henry V ultimately turns his anxiety into a joke, seeing the link between his "father's ambition" and "civil wars" as the cause of his "aspect of iron" that frightens Kate (5.2.225–28).

II

Most readers find Henry V's soliloquy in act 4, scene 1, an extraordinarily powerful moment. The crucial questions it poses for interpretation are: what is the place of the soliloquy in the play as a whole? how do we experience the remainder of the play? how are we to understand the king's turning from meditation to battle—"The day, my friends, and all things wait for me" (4.1.309)? One response is to treat the soliloquy in isolation—as a fleeting, inward glimpse that underscores precisely what we do not find elsewhere in the play. J. Dover Wilson, however, has demonstrated the possibility of integrating the soliloquy into the ongoing action, seeing it as a part of a continuous sequence of Henry V's development and growth. In particular, the soliloquy is a spiritual crisis that not only humanizes but tests and strengthens him, enabling him to face the upcoming battle with "the ultimate heroic faith."[8] My own view is that Henry V's heroic faith remains problematic and that Shakespeare does not ask for simple assent to it, but Wilson is right in not splitting the soliloquy off from the rest of the play. There are several dramatic elements in the final section of *Henry V* that are integrally connected with the emotions emerging in the king's soliloquy.

The encounter with Henry IV's guilt is not simply left behind, but actively suppressed. The emphatic vision of blood brotherhood following Henry V's soliloquy dissolves and evades the burden of paternal sin:

> We would not die in that man's company
> That fears his fellowship to die with us. . . .
> We few, we happy few, we band of brothers;
> For he to-day that sheds his blood with me
> Shall be my brother.
>
> (4.3.38–39, 60–62)

The quality of elation in this speech can be explained in part by the way its stress on male fellowship takes the pressure off the father–son tension enacted in act 4, scene 1.[9] The "band of brothers" gains its cohesiveness from being selective as well as nonhierarchical: "And gentlemen in England, now a-bed, / Shall think themselves accurs'd they were not here; / And hold their manhoods cheap" (64–66). Ironically, such sacrificial brotherhood has the potential to restore harmony across generations: "This story shall the good man teach his son" (4.3.56).

The particular point in the play that answers to the emotional power of Henry V's story of brotherhood sanctified by bloodshed is the mutual death of York and Suffolk recounted by Exeter in act 4, scene 6. Earlier, Henry V's anticipation of heroic death and fame had included a macabre strain:

> And those that leave their valiant bones in France,
> Dying like men, though buried in your dunghills,
> They shall be fam'd; for there the sun shall greet
>   them,
> And draw their honors reeking up to heaven,
> Leaving their earthly parts to choke your clime,
> The smell whereof shall breed a plague in France.
>   (4.3.98–103)

Now the grotesque details are sublimated in the fraternal ascension to chronicle heaven:

> Suffolk first died; and York, all haggled over,
> Comes to him, where in gore he lay insteeped,
> And takes him by the beard, kisses the gashes
> That bloodily did yawn upon his face.
> He cries aloud, "Tarry, my cousin Suffolk!
> My soul shall thine keep company to heaven;
> Tarry, sweet soul, for mine, then fly abreast,
> As in this glorious and well-foughten field
> We kept together in our chivalry!"
>   (4.6.11–19)

At the moment of heroic death, when integration with the rest of one's life is moot, the guard against the normally dreaded effeminacy can be set aside. Expression of affection is compatible with manliness because "honor-owing wounds" (9) are felt to be affirmed by York's embraces.

This ideal of collaborative manhood receives its confirmation when Henry V joins Exeter in indulging in an emotional response to the story:

> EXE.   The pretty and sweet manner of it forc'd
> Those waters from me which I would have stopp'd;
> But I had not so much of man in me,
> And all my mother came into mine eyes
> And gave me up to tears.
> KING.   I blame you not;
> For hearing this, I must perforce compound
> With mistful eyes, or they will issue too.
> But hark, what new alarum is this same?
>   (4.6.28–35)

Henry V's vicarious participation is sharply curtailed as he is immediately called away to demonstrate once more his toughness. Nonetheless, a moment is long enough to secure the king's approval of this heroic male tenderness. In the company of trusted men, the "mother" can be let out briefly to bear witness to men's quasi-maternal cherishing of one another. The kiss which "epous'd" York to death and to Suffolk and which "seal'd / A testament of noble-ending love" (25–27) is, in its way, moving; but finally it is unsatisfying because too satisfying.

From our perspective, the witness's allusion to "the pretty and sweet manner of it" (4.6.28) refers not only to the incident but also to his telling of it. This phrase indicates Shakespeare's ability critically to place such an episode of idealized male comradeship. In *Henry V*, Shakespeare is not simply victimized by the sentimental dream of self-contained masculine purity; rather, he consciously dramatizes this dream.[10] The narrative frame and style of act 4, scene 6, convey an overly precious, cloying, pseudo-archaic tone that allows Shakespeare to present the chivalric ideal exemplified by the York–Suffolk story as anachronistic convention.[11] The York–Suffolk set piece is a microcosm of the historical as well as psychological escapism implicit in Henry V's heroic impulse.

In the second tetralogy, two historical frames of reference are superimposed: the period 1399–1420, which is the most obvious content of the plays, is implicitly seen from the vantage point of 1595–99, the time of actual composition. As Shakespeare's use of the history play becomes more sophisticated, he shows increasing awareness of the distinction and conflict between medieval and Renaissance cultural modes. In *England in the Late Middle Ages* A. R. Myers sees that time as "a changing world" in which there is a "widening gulf between professed aims and reality":

Take, for instance, the ideas of chivalry; its feats of heroism in single combat, its crusades and adventures, its code of feudal loyalty and courtly love were appropriate to the feudal order, but by the end of the thirteenth century this had lost its vitality. Yet the militant aristocracy of the late middle ages professed to find in chivalry its guiding principles, and the chroniclers who, like Froissart, wrote to please noble patrons echoed their beliefs. The outward forms of chivalry remained and flourished; tournaments and trappings of chivalry became more splendid, chivalrous courtesy and etiquette became stricter and more complex, orders of knighthood increased in number and pomp. But in human relationships, especially those of rulers, the spirit of chivalry was dying; by the late fifteenth century the crusading impulse, for example, was dead, though kings like Edward IV and Henry VII could still pay lip service to it.[12]

Henry V enacts this tension between the "outward forms" and the "dead spirit" of chivalry. By the time of *Henry V*, Shakespeare has made a fundamental shift of perspective. The pursuit and attainment of honor is no longer considered an exemplary thing in itself but rather as a function of some other context, in particular, the contexts of political skill and conscience. In the new perspective, monolithic commitment to chivalric heroism is seen as anachronistic and reductive (as in the earlier instance of Hotspur).

The other side of this attenuated chivalric coin is the Dauphin, whose mistress is his horse (3.7.42). In the parallel scene to the York–Suffolk apotheosis, the defeated Dauphin draws the appropriate conclusions about his "everlasting shame" (4.5.4). *Henry V*, like *1 Henry VI*, portrays a sharp contrast between the English and the French, a contrast turning on manliness and the lack of it. Talbot in *1 Henry VI* exemplifies the approved image of manhood based on resistance to women and on allegiance to men. Henry V in a more complex way continues this tradition. The English/French contrast in *Henry V* makes possible two separate centers of male comradeship—one legitimate and manly, the other its opposite. Herein lies the value of the Dauphin as a travesty of masculinity. His laughable presence diverts and exorcises fears of effeminacy: the English tenderness imaged by York and Suffolk must be virile because the French—epitomized by the Dauphin—are so patently effete.

Yet the Dauphin is paired in rivalry with Henry V. Since one's greatness is measured by the stature of one's rivals, Henry V appears to be mismatched with the Dauphin, who threatens to lower the king to his level (as he cannot be raised to the king's). In their bondedness, rivals mirror each other: the Dauphin casts a bad image on Henry V against which the latter's oratory proves an inadequate defense. Prior to his predictable humiliation, the Dauphin plays a stronger role than his actual weakness would lead us to expect. Like Hotspur (*1H4*, 5.2.69–71), the Dauphin is fooled by Hal's disguise as a wastrel (*H5*, 1.2.250–53). The fact that the Dauphin is an amusingly ineffectual version of Hotspur is part of the dramatic point. The Dauphin forces Henry V to reassert in stronger terms his original strategy of holiday surprise:

> And like bright metal on a sullen ground,
> My reformation, glitt'ring o'er my fault,
> Shall show more goodly and attract more eyes
> Than that which hath no foil to set it off.
> (*1H4*, 1.2.212–15)

>   And we understand him well,
> How he comes o'er us with our wilder days,
> Not measuring what use we made of them. . . .
> For that I have laid by my majesty
> And plodded like a man for working-days;
> But I will rise there with so full a glory
> That I will dazzle all the eyes of France,
> Yea, strike the Dolphin blind to look on us.
> (*H5*, 1.2.266–68, 276–80)

The Dauphin is a "foil" who arouses a depth of anger out of proportion to his provision of a target to satisfy it. The disparity between the Dauphin's taunt with the tennis balls and Henry V's overwrought counterattack (259–97) embarrasses the king, making it appear that the Dauphin's frivolous gesture has hit a tender nerve. The king can remove his rival's threat only by silencing him, yet no direct encounter parallel to that between Hal and Hotspur in *1 Henry IV* is hazarded. Instead, the Dauphin simply vanishes, his place as son taken over by Henry V.

In his battle rhetoric, the king envisages two images of father–son relations. His heroic appeal to his own men presupposes an ideal harmony:

> On, on, you noblest English,
> Whose blood is fet from fathers of war-proof!
> Fathers that, like so many Alexanders,
> Have in these parts from morn till even fought. . . .
>   now attest
> That those whom you call'd fathers did beget you.
>   (3.1.17–20, 22–23)

The obverse, his threatening the French with family destruction, countenances aggression against the father: "Your fathers taken by the silver beards, / And their most reverend heads dash'd to the walls" (3.3.36–37). This double image of the father is embodied specifically in Henry V's contrasting attitudes toward Henry IV and the king of France.

As a father–son pair, the French king and the Dauphin serve the same function as Northumberland and Hotspur by offering a corrupted, negative version of the bond between Henry IV and Hal. The anger, doubt, and criticism that Henry V feels toward his father in the despairing soliloquy of act 4, scene 1, are stifled.[13] But these same feelings can be directed without reservation toward the king of France, whose enfeebled position invites scorn. At the same time, Henry V can punish his own illicit parricidal impulses by casting the Dauphin in the role of the undependable bad son who deserves to be beaten.

Prompted by the tennis balls, Henry V takes self-righteous pleasure in blaming his attack on the father on the unreliable son's misbehavior: "We will in France, by God's grace, play a set / Shall strike his father's crown into the hazard"; "God before, / We'll chide this Dolphin at his father's door" (1.2.262–63, 307–8). In the final scene, Henry V relishes his control over the French king when he blandly assures Katherine that her father will approve their marriage: "Nay, it will please him well, Kate; it shall please him" (5.2.248–49). Henry V insists on his formal titles as son and heir to the French king (335–42) partly because it makes legitimate his psychological diplomacy:

FRANCE.   Nor this I have not, brother, so denied,
             But your request shall make me let it pass.
HEN.   I pray you then, in love and dear alliance,
             Let that one article rank with the rest,
             And thereupon give me your daughter.
FRANCE.   Take her, fair son, and from her blood raise up
             Issue to me.

                                            (343–49)

The French king's inevitable yielding establishes a protocol whereby Henry V resolves the contradictory actions of conquering the father and of being accepted harmoniously as his rightful successor. Making his submission complete, the French king calls Henry V not "brother" (343) but "fair son" (348). The father he has ignominiously defeated thus transforms this conquest into a saccharine vision of peace—"and this dear conjunction / Plant neighborhood and Christian-like accord / In their sweet bosoms, that never war advance / His bleeding sword 'twixt England and fair France" (5.2.352–55). How unrealistic this fantasy of unity Henry V elicits, the final chorus soon reminds us.

In the concluding scene the characters try to play a comedy. Burgundy sets the stage by pulling out comic stops reminiscent of the recovery from pastoral disorder in *A Midsummer Night's Dream* (2.1.82–117). Recounting the chaos in nature created by war (*H5*, 5.2.38–62), Burgundy imagines the restoration of the "Dear nurse of art, plenties, and joyful births" that could make "Our fertile

France" once again the "best garden of the world" (35–37). This general pattern of comic denouement is reinforced by conspicuous allusion to the convention equating closure with wedding. The play ends with a performance of epithalamic blessing:

> God, the best maker of all marriages,
> Combine your hearts in one, your realms in one!
> As man and wife, being two are one in love,
> So be there 'twixt your kingdoms such a spousal,
> That never may ill office, or fell jealousy,
> Which troubles oft the bed of blessed marriage. . . .
>
> (359–64)

Yet we are prevented from taking full comic satisfaction in this marital hopefulness not only because the chorus throws cold water on the political harmony it envisions but also because the actual courtship we have witnessed is not an unqualified success.

Henry V applies himself to wooing with a gusto appropriate to comic decorum. His inability "to mince it in love" (5.2.126) and his plain speaking are often taken as evidence of an engaging bluntness. Yet the language barrier creates difficulty as well as humor. Kate's role as unresponsive straw woman blocks the quick conclusion Harry seeks—"Give me your answer, i' faith, do, and so clap hands and a bargain" (129–30). Though he maintains an unflappable, upbeat tone, his bravado becomes repetitious, his "downright oaths" (144) feeling less and less funny and enjoyable. He seems reduced to a "fellow of infinite tongue" (156), who keeps "wearing out his suit" (128–29). As elsewhere in the play, Henry V is here forced to talk too much, endlessly to justify himself.

The emphatic soldier identity (5.2.99, 149, 166) that the king brings to the courtship undermines as much as it promotes a comic spirit. He looks beyond wooing to the son this marriage can produce to carry on Christian military exploits, thereby turning Kate into "a good soldier-breeder" (206). The tension between political opportunity and love has been present from the outset. The king's marriage does not depend on the outcome of the private wooing scene since, as he announces, his power to enforce his desires is guaranteed in advance: "She is our capital demand, compris'd / Within the fore-rank of our articles" (96–97). This externally imposed conclusion casts some doubt on the status of Henry V's love by raising the possibility that mechanical appropriation substitutes for, rather than coincides with, genuine feeling. But the king's love is also subject to question on internal grounds.

The ultimate reason for the deep awkwardness beneath the comic surface in the courtship scene comes from the way Henry V's "speaking plain soldier" (5.2.149) causes him to portray sexuality as a form of military aggression and conquest. Phrases like "I love thee cruelly" and "I get thee with scambling" (202–3, 204–5) contain ironies the king cannot control.[14] The exuberant mixing of love and war comes naturally to Henry V:

> If I could win a lady at leap-frog, or by vaulting into my saddle with my armor on my back, under the correction of bragging be it spoken, I should quickly leap into a wife. Or if I might buffet for my love, or bound my horse for her favors, I could lay on like a butcher, and sit like a jack-an-apes, never off.
> (136–42)

The issue here is not bragging but the metaphorical equation of woman with horse, an equation the Dauphin has taught us: "O then belike she was old and gentle, and you rode like a kern of Ireland, your French hose off, and in your straight strossers" (3.7.52–54). Henry V's wooing in the final scene implicitly culminates his rivalry with the Dauphin, which had a sexual current from the start in the challenge presented by the tennis balls. One does not need the conflict between the clowns—"Pistol's cock is up" (2.1.52)—to alert us to the phallic implication of the king's conversion of "balls to gun-stones" (1.2.282). The sexual reference of "the Paris balls" is confirmed by the threat of war that puns on lover: "He'll make your Paris

Louvre shake for it, / Were it the mistress court of mighty Europe" (2.4.131–33).

The French anticipate their defeat in sexual terms:

> Our madams mock at us, and plainly say
> Our mettle is bred out, and they will give
> Their bodies to the lust of English youth
> To new-store France with bastard warriors.
> (3.5.28–31)

> Let him go hence, and with his cap in hand
> Like a base pander hold the chamber-door
> Whilst by a slave, no gentler than my dog,
> His fairest daughter is contaminated.
> (4.5.13–16)

Henry V's wartime oratory had promised no less (3.3.11–14, 20–21, 33–35), while his peacetime approach holds this threat in abeyance as in the elaborate banter likening Katherine to French cities "all girdled with maiden walls that war hath never ent'red" (5.2.321–23). The king's coarseness in the wooing scene loses much of its comic appeal because it participates in the troubled sexuality displayed throughout the play. The "frankness" of Henry V's "mirth" (291) is finally a sexual humor that can be shared only by men, as his turning to Burgundy for support suggests: "Yet they do wink and yield, as love is blind and enforces" (300–1). The enmity between French and English men is in part resolved because they can unite in erotic humor at Katherine's expense.

The second tetralogy of English history plays avoids the threat to male rule that formidable women present in the first tetralogy by restricting women to the periphery. In *Richard II*, the Duchess of Gloucester and Richard's queen can complain or lament but cannot genuinely threaten. The Duchess of York is neutralized by being treated as a source of comedy. Richard, who sees himself in relation to his kingdom as a "mother with her child" (3.2.8), is himself eliminated in favor of the apparently more promising masculinity of Bolingbroke. The women in the *Henry IV* plays have an even more marginal existence. The spirited wit and brusque affection in Hotspur's relationship with Kate are relatively insignificant given his clear statement of priorities:

> This is no world
> To play with mammets and to tilt with lips.
> We must have bloody noses and crack'd crowns,
> And pass them current too. God's me, my horse!
> (*1H4*, 2.3.91–94)

The emphasis on chivalric warfare rather than chivalric love applies even more so to Hal, who participates in the convention of masculine purity automatically because he is not compromised by any connections to a woman. For the purposes of the second tetralogy, Hal is not "of woman born." Coppélia Kahn convincingly argues that Hal's association with Falstaff "represents the wish to bypass women."[15] In this regard, the similarity between Falstaff and the wifeless Henry IV makes Hal's transition from one to the other relatively easy. Hal's reunion with his father continues to fulfill the need to bypass women; the rejection of Falstaff and the reconciliation with Henry IV in no way disrupts Hal-Henry V's commitment to male bonding.

The ending of *Henry V* proposes to round out the king's character by providing him with a woman, but this proposal cannot be enacted because his character is too entrenched in a narrow masculinity. All emotional depth is concentrated in male relations. Henry V's attempt to conclude a relationship with Katherine in the final scene is the exception that proves the general rule.[16] The residual awkwardness of the king's wooing of Kate cannot be attributed simply to inexperience with women, nor can it be joked away because there is a more specific obstacle: the counterpull of male bonding, whose strength has been affirmed by the consummation allowed to York and

Suffolk. When we compare the "testament of noble-ending love" (4.6.27) offered by York and Suffolk with the king's courtship of Katherine, the two love scenes cannot compete; the power of the earlier instance overshadows the final scene, which seems unfulfilled by comparison. The entire second tetralogy stands behind a military definition of masculinity that cannot be overturned by a last-minute ending.

III

The usual way to make the transition from *Henry V* to *Hamlet* is to link Henry V with Fortinbras.[17] This linkage expresses the view that Henry V is reduced to the political function that he performs so efficiently. A much richer and more accurate way to make the connection is to place Henry V directly in the line that leads to Hamlet. Both young men are poised between two father figures. Each has little or no difficulty in distinguishing and rejecting the false, usurping father. Though he makes use of Falstaff for strategic purposes, Hal is clear from the beginning about his ability to banish him. Claudius, like Falstaff, is a Lord of Misrule who is to be rejected as a politically subversive abuser of holiday festivity. While waiting for the ghost's appearance, Hamlet bitterly criticizes Claudius's drinking as an inappropriate "observance" of "custom" (1.4.16, 15). In both instances it is paradoxically the relationship with the rightful father that the sons find impossible to resolve.

For Hal and Hamlet, it is a problem to experience the declaration that invigorates Orlando: "The spirit of my father grows strong in me." Orlando, who is not forced to deal with the original father, easily secures a benevolent substitute in Duke Senior. For Hal and Hamlet, however, identity is formed and given permanent shape in a decisive encounter with the father. Hal's role is thrust upon him when, at the end of *2 Henry IV*, the dying king not only bequeaths his power but also specifies how his son is to use the kingship. Similarly, the ghost defines Hamlet's destiny. The highly charged confrontation scene is characterized by a mixture of intimacy and distance, by the father's melodramatic anger as well as his melodramatic love. The father urgently challenges and claims the son's love, and this urgency is complicated by the father's insistence on his own deficiencies, which the son is called upon to remedy. Like Cordelia, Henry V and Hamlet "go about their father's business" as well as their own. Ultimately, the paternal injunction is a painful burden for Henry V as well as for Hamlet. Like Cordelia, they become "sacrifices" to their father's idealized visions of vindication and redemption. But, unlike Cordelia, the two men are not silent about their fate.

A sharp contrast between Henry V as a man of action and Hamlet as a man of thought is misleading because both are primarily men of long speeches. In each case, the long speech symbolizes a continual search for a justifiable identity. The urgency of self-definition is intensified by a conscience based on atonement with the father. In both *Henry V* and *Hamlet*, the pressure of the father's demands is manifested in the son's self-conscious acting. Like Hamlet, Hal has put on an antic disposition, which then becomes a lasting problem because the act cannot be discontinued at will. Hal as Henry V is a player king who unsuccessfully attempts to stage situations that will give his identity complete credibility.

The continuity between *Henry V* and *Hamlet* appears in other ways as well. The disturbed relationship between men and women exemplified in the Henry V–Katherine courtship anticipates the more overt instance of Hamlet and Ophelia. Henry V's image of male bonding between brothers as an alternative to the problematic tension of father–son relations—an image crystallized in the York–Suffolk scene—connects with Hamlet's reliance on the faithful comrade Horatio, to whom in the final scene he entrusts his story. Both Henry V and Hamlet are poised between the two incompatible options of male and heterosexual ties. In both cases, forms of male bonding take precedence at the expense of relations with women. *Hamlet* more directly confronts alienation from women, but the ending of *Henry V*, in raising yet not fulfilling festive marital expectations, reveals the problem. In thus helping to prepare the way for *Hamlet*'s treatment of male–male and male–female relations, *Henry V* should be viewed not as an artistic backwater in Shakespeare's development but as part of the mainstream.[18] To acknowledge the central position of *Henry V* as the link between the second tetralogy and *Hamlet,* we must see that the play cuts deeper than Henry V's military success and gives dramatic weight to his psychological complexity.

Henry V dramatizes the gap between the received story and the identity that actually emerges.[19] Henry V tries rhetorically to close the gap between expectations and actuality; his failure to do so means that identity becomes an open question, as happens more spectacularly in the tragedies. The relentless quality of Henry V's language comes from the stressfulness of this irreducible gap. It is as though he keeps redoing the image he projects in the speeches in an effort to make it come out right. But validation of identity through chronicle eludes him because his identity is too heterogeneous to fit the epic image. Hence, Henry V is placed in a tragic condition despite the lack of a catastrophic tragic denouement. It is left to the final chorus, from its perspective outside the dramatic action, to strike a tragic note.

· 3 ·

Maternal Images and Male Bonds
in *Hamlet, Othello,* and *King Lear*

The role of male bonding in each of these three major
tragedies varies. Central to the dramatic action of *Hamlet* is
the privileged status accorded to the male bond enacted by
Hamlet and Horatio; in different ways *Othello* and *King Lear*
subsequently qualify the status of such bonds. Initially, the
Hamlet–Horatio relationship seems not only unpromising
but irrelevant. Renunciation of the "fellow student"
(1.2.177) from Wittenberg is a precondition for contact with
the ghost as Hamlet must break away from Horatio to "follow" (1.4.63, 68, 79, 86): "It beckons you to go away with
it, / As if it some impartment did desire / To you alone"
(58–60). Accepting the isolation that allegiance to his
"father's spirit" (1.5.9) imposes on him, Hamlet refuses to
confide in Horatio:

HOR.	What news, my lord?
HAM.	O, wonderful.
HOR.	Good my lord, tell it.
HAM.	No, you will reveal it.
	(116–18)

Though he professes his "love and friending to you"
(185), Hamlet's "wild and whirling words" (133) constitute an evasive action that puts Horatio off and asserts
Hamlet's distance: "There are more things in heaven and
earth, Horatio, / Than are dreamt of in your philosophy"
(166–67).

However, after this inauspicious beginning, we learn
that Hamlet has taken Horatio into his confidence: "One

scene of it comes near the circumstance / Which I have told thee of my father's death" (3.2.76–77). He also takes Horatio into his heart:

> Give me that man
> That is not passion's slave, and I will wear him
> In my heart's core, ay, in my heart of heart,
> As I do thee.
>
> (71–74)

So fervent and unexpected is this declaration that Hamlet is made to break off from it with: "Something too much of this" (74).[1] It is almost as though Shakespeare as well as Hamlet is embarrassed by the force of Hamlet's feeling, as though an impropriety had occurred. In the immediate circumstances the subject is dropped and Horatio allowed no opportunity to respond. Nevertheless, the play continues to draw on the "Something too much" of this male tie, so much so that the final scene depends heavily on it. The importance of Horatio to Hamlet lies in the prospect he offers of an alternative to unresolvable relationships to the ghost, to Gertrude, and to Ophelia.

I

The tensions in the relationship between father and son in the *Henriad* are pushed in *Hamlet* to the point of full-fledged, paralyzing crisis. The patriarchal imperative equates love with obedience; love not being granted unconditionally, the son proves his loyalty by performing his duty as the father sees it. In Hamlet's case, this test takes the most drastic form imaginable:

GHOST. If thou didst ever thy dear father love—
HAM. O God!
GHOST. Revenge his foul and most unnatural murther.
(1.5.23–25)

Hamlet's reaction to the ghost's demand is to transform his mind into a tabula rasa fit to record the father's total claim on the son: "And thy commandement all alone shall live / Within the book and volume of my brain, / Unmix'd with baser matter" (102–4). At first sight the ghost appears to be a perfect solution to Hamlet's alienation because its intervention restores a direct link to the patriarchal heritage on which Hamlet might base a heroic identity. But the ghost is ultimately part of Hamlet's problem.[2] While the ghost bolsters Hamlet's identity by confirming the validity of his "prophetic soul" (40), it simultaneously takes away identity by usurping Hamlet's self. One reason for Hamlet's later defensiveness toward Rosencrantz and Guildenstern, who so consistently demonstrate their inability to "play upon" Hamlet, is his prior experience with a ghost who has rendered him "easier to be play'd on than a pipe" (3.2.370) and who has even perhaps "plucked out the heart of my mystery" (365–66).

The ghost's takeover of Hamlet's identity denies options. The distinction between "To be, or not to be" (3.1.55) is hard to maintain when the self-fashioning the ghost requires entails self-cancellation—the loss of independence. Hamlet must respond to his father's love, but at the same time he must be acutely sensitive to the coercive, all-encompassing nature of the self his father has fashioned for him. Hence a conflict emerges in Hamlet between obedience and resistance to the ghost's demands.[3] Under the pressure of the ghost's "Remember me" (1.5.91) Hamlet makes an overwhelming commitment to obedience. Yet in the outburst that ends the scene—"O cursed spite / That ever I was born to set it right" (188–89)—Hamlet sounds the note of regret that includes a potential for resistance. It is in connection with this inner conflict that Horatio's value to Hamlet can be understood.

When Hamlet abruptly reaches out to Horatio, he is establishing a point of contact outside the distressed father–son relationship. He alleviates his isolation by choosing a man who is "not a pipe for Fortune's finger / To sound what stop she please" (3.2.70–71), that is, a man who offers the security of a constancy that contrasts with Hamlet's own experience of being played upon by the ghost. Hamlet immediately presses the alliance with Horatio into the service of the ghost, sharing his triumph when Horatio and Hamlet remain on stage after Claudius's hasty exit from the play within a play: "O good Horatio, I'll take the ghost's word for a thousand pound. Didst perceive?" (286–87). Nevertheless, Hamlet's friendship with Horatio is not entirely contained within the framework of Hamlet's allegiance to his father. As the friendship is developed, it becomes a relationship unto itself, separate from Hamlet's overriding concern with the ghost.

Horatio serves as a refuge for Hamlet not only because he provides momentary relief from anguish but also because he occasions a sense of trust through which Hamlet might recover a portion of the identity negated by his submission to the ghost. One reading of *Hamlet* flatly pronounces Hamlet's failure to maintain any independence. In this view, Hamlet finally capitulates to the ghost's demands.[4] It is true that Hamlet does not achieve complete "success" in separating himself from his father: his use of the signet (5.2.49) indicates a continuing identification with his father's purposes. But it is also true that while Hamlet does in the end carry out the ghost's "dread command" (3.4.108) by murdering Claudius, his identity does not thereby reduce simply to the embodiment of his father's dictates. The conflict between the role his father imposes on him and the separate self toward which he gropes does not collapse in favor of the former. Hamlet is ultimately true to himself in the sense that he holds on to his dilemma. The conflict itself enables him tragically to establish an individual identity, a process that helps to account for his serenity at the end. Hamlet's struggle redeems the deeper resonance in Polonius's precept "to thine own self be true" (1.3.78), one of the saws Hamlet tried to "wipe away" (1.5.99) under the impact of the ghost's revelation. In making the "truth" of Hamlet's "self" dramatically convincing, Horatio is essential.

Horatio's prominence toward the end of the play coincides with the cessation of Hamlet's soliloquies. Hamlet's last soliloquy occurs in act 4, scene 4; Horatio is at Hamlet's side throughout act 5. By addressing his final statements to Horatio, Hamlet is freed from his verbal isolation, especially from his earlier self-torturing relation to language as one who "Must like a whore unpack my heart with words" (2.2.585). Having in Horatio a personal audience he can count on to receive his words and ultimately to carry on his linguistic future after his own "silence" (5.2.358) allows Hamlet to feel that language is no longer automatically inadequate to "that within" (1.2.85). The Hamlet–Horatio relationship provides one of the main lines of development from act 4, scene 6, where Hamlet reestablishes contact with Horatio by letter, through to the final scene, when Hamlet asks his faithful comrade "To tell my story" (5.2.349). The letter serves as a point of transition between Hamlet's soliloquies and the direct contact with Horatio that begins in the graveyard. In closing the letter by presenting himself as "He that thou knowest thine" (4.6.30), Hamlet reiterates his earlier "election" (3.2.64) of Horatio and sets the tone for the intimate address that his devotion will make possible in the final act.

Despite Hamlet's absolute dedication to the ghost's final order to "remember me" (1.5.91), the ghost does not have the last word. Horatio's presence acts as an alternative that allows Hamlet to expand his attention beyond a narrow focus on the ghost. In the context of the final scene, other competing considerations enter in that dilute, if not displace, the monolithic emphasis on revenge. Hamlet remembers his father only intermittently at the end of the play, and he remembers other things with greater emotional force. In particular, he is concerned with attending to his own memorial. By directing Horatio to "report me and my cause aright / To the unsatisfied" (5.2.339–40), he acts to commemorate himself, thus creating a wedge between his father's story and his own. The two Hamlets are not synonymous. Our final image of Hamlet as "sweet prince" (359) contrasts with the initial picture of the father as the archaic epic hero who "smote the sledded Polacks on the ice" (1.1.63); we value the difference partly because it costs Hamlet so dearly.

Horatio's collaboration is indispensable in effecting this difference between father and son, as the structure of the last scene emphasizes. The long exchange, beginning with the appeal "Horatio, I am dead" (5.2.338), comprises Hamlet's prominently positioned, final action. Speaking directly to his dead friend, Horatio acknowledges Hamlet's special identity as "sweet prince," thereby healing his "wounded name" (344) and granting the "felicity" (347) for which he had hoped: "Good night, sweet prince, / And flights of angels sing thee to thy rest!" (359–60). Some commentators conclude from Horatio's subsequent public rhetoric—"And let me speak to th' yet unknowing world / How these things came about. So you shall hear" (379–80)—that he will be an untrustworthy witness to Hamlet's inner story. But it is worth noting that Hamlet too uses the melodramatic voice when addressing a larger public: "You that look pale, and tremble at this chance, / That are but mutes or audience to this act" (334–35). It is the private exchange between Hamlet and Horatio that counts. Despite the reserve implied by Horatio's demurral that Hamlet "considers too curiously" (5.1.206), Horatio's capacity for intimacy is sufficient to make dramatically plausible and compelling his bond with Hamlet. He is there when Hamlet needs him: "If thou didst ever hold me in thy heart, / Absent thee from felicity a while" (5.2.346–47). Hamlet's plea to his friend recapitulates the ghost's heart-rending summons: "If thou didst ever thy dear father love" (1.5.23). But there is a difference. The play's final scene contrasts two versions of the transmission of heritage. Hamlet inherits from the ghost the obligation to revenge, which is consummated in the final scene. At the same time, Hamlet bequeaths his story to Horatio, thus preserving an alternate legacy of nonviolent fraternal cherishing. To bring out the limitations of the affection expressed in the Hamlet–Horatio bond, let us turn to Hamlet's relations with women.

Horatio has a double function in the play since he provides Hamlet with an alternative not only to the hectoring ghost but also to the crucial women in his life, Gertrude and Ophelia. Gertrude's exposed position in the play contrasts with the marginal maternal presence in *Henry V*. Isabel, the queen of France, renders herself invisible in the final scene by accommodating the wishes of the conquering hero, whose needs she places above those of her husband and her daughter. She facilitates Henry V's peace: "Happily a woman's voice may do some good,/ When articles too nicely urg'd may be stood upon" (5.2.93–94). She yields Katherine to his wooing: "She hath good leave" (98). She ratifies their marriage in the most flattering rhetoric: "God, the best maker of all marriages, / Combine your hearts in one!" (359–60). Gertrude has far greater visibility in *Hamlet* partly because she is deprived of this conventional maternal role when she sponsors marital love: "And for your part, Ophelia, I do wish / That your good beauties be the happy cause / Of Hamlet's wildness" (3.1.37–39).

Faced with the fact of Ophelia's death, Gertrude poignantly recognizes the denial of her "wish": "I hop'd thou shouldst have been my Hamlet's wife. / I thought thy bride-bed to have deck'd, sweet maid, / And not have strew'd thy grave" (5.1.244–46). But long before these "maimed rites" (219) for Ophelia, Gertrude is aware that her son's affections are not directed toward the younger woman and that she herself is a major cause of his "wildness": "I doubt it is no other but the main, / His father's death and our o'erhasty marriage" (2.2.56–57). If Isabel performs a disappearing act in *Henry V* by blending with the hero's desires, Gertrude stands out because her remarriage calls attention to her own separate desires, desires that Hamlet finds painful to contemplate but nevertheless feels compelled to track down in lurid detail in his mother's closet. The "something" "rotten in the state of Denmark" (1.4.90) leads directly, through the ghost's metaphor, to the degraded sexuality in which Gertrude is trapped: "So lust, though to a radiant angel link'd, / Will sate itself in a celestial bed / And prey on garbage" (1.5.55–57). On this point, father and son agree: in his opening soliloquy Hamlet has already lamented his mother's sexual "frailty" (1.2.146).

Lacking a mother within the play, Laertes is forced to invent one to give full expression to the family integrity he defends:

> That drop of blood that's calm proclaims me bastard,
> Cries cuckold to my father, brands the harlot
> Even here between the chaste unsmirched brow
> Of my true mother.
>
> (4.5.118–21)

By contrast, Hamlet renounces calmness because his "true mother" has made herself a "harlot" through remarriage and made him a "bastard" by dispossessing him of the maternal inheritance to which he feels entitled.[5] His mourning is for loss of her as well as of his father. Hamlet makes a desperate effort to reverse the effects of Gertrude's marriage to Claudius and to recover her original "chaste unsmirched brow": "go not to my uncle's bed" (3.4.159). But the ideal image with which Hamlet harangues his mother is never restored in her. In the end, despite her generous gesture to him—"Here, Hamlet, take my napkin, rub thy brows. / The Queen carouses to thy fortune, Hamlet" (5.2.288–89)—he dismisses her with an unfeeling "Wretched queen, adieu!" (333), while putting himself in Horatio's care.

His actual mother having failed him, Hamlet finds an image of his "true mother" in the speech he selects for the player's recitation.[6] The second half of this "passionate speech" (2.2.432) is as important as the first, as Hamlet's prompting indicates: "Say on, come to Hecuba" (501). Hecuba's maternal identity is established by the reference to " 'her lank and all o'er-teemed loins' " (508). Despite the exhaustion of child bearing, her capacity for grief is inexhaustible. Her " 'bisson rheum' " (506) contrasts sharply with Gertrude's false tears: "Ere yet the salt of most unrighteous tears / Had left the flushing in her galled eyes, / She married" (1.2.154–56). So great is Hecuba's sorrow that it is envisaged as inducing a sympathetic response in the cosmos, the gods themselves holding up the mirror to her maternal nature:

> "The instant burst of clamor that she made,
> Unless things mortal move them not at all,
> Would have made milch the burning eyes of heaven,
> And passion in the gods."
>
> (2.2.515–18)

The imagery connects tears and milk, suggesting that the literal nurturance of the mother's breast is the epitome and source of compassionate feeling.[7]

Her lust having disqualified Gertrude in Hamlet's eyes, she is unavailable to satisfy this nurturant image. By offering a comforting, solicitous presence for Hamlet, Horatio partially fills this need. In addition, Hamlet himself takes on the Hecuba image in his subsequent soliloquy:

> What's Hecuba to him, or he to Hecuba,
> That he should weep for her? What would he do
> Had he the motive and cue for passion
> That I have? He would drown the stage with tears.
>
> (2.2.559–62)

Like Lucrece, Hamlet finds in Hecuba a face "where all distress and dolor dwell'd" (*Lucrece*, 1446)—an image adequate to his own extreme experience. Like Lucrece, he "shapes his sorrow to the beldame's woes" (*Lucrece*, 1458). Together Hamlet and Horatio incorporate into their bond the compassion for which Hecuba is the model. But this compassionate use of the male bond is not fully satisfactory, for Hamlet's companionship with Horatio is less an alternative than a substitute for the original bond with his mother. As an attempt to do without the more highly charged maternal bond, the male bond, though moving, has a more limited emotional range.

We are thus reminded that Hamlet's investment in Horatio results from his failure to resolve his relations with Gertrude or Ophelia, both of whom arouse (and potentially could have fulfilled) a more intense need. Similarly, Othello turns to Iago only after the deeper bond with Desdemona fails, and Lear turns to male support only when he cannot have Cordelia. But even in disillusionment both men maintain their primary focus on the woman. Iago's difficulty in keeping Othello on the course of revenge—"But yet the pity of it, Iago! O, Iago, the pity of it, Iago!" (4.1.195–96)—suggests Othello's continuing attachment to the Desdemona he thinks he has lost. For Lear, everything hinges on Cordelia: "This feather stirs, she lives! If it be so, / It is a chance which does redeem all sorrows / That ever I have felt" (5.3.266–68). In Hamlet's case, however, the severance of ties to women is permanent; virtually all affection is transferred to Horatio.

The Hamlet–Horatio bond bespeaks a self-sufficiency that dissociates itself too readily from connections with women, as when Hamlet jokes about Osric's manners while feeding at the breast—" 'A did comply, sir, with his dug before 'a suck'd it" (5.2.187–88)—or when he discounts his hesitation about the match with Laertes as "such a kind of gain-giving, as would perhaps trouble a woman" (215–16). The undercurrent of contempt for women and for dependence on them in these casual remarks had earlier been expressed with full force in the misogynist rage by which Hamlet ends his vulnerability to Ophelia.

Of course Hamlet has no monopoly on abuse of Ophelia, as Polonius's treatment of his daughter as an object to be exploited for his own needs shows. Polonius expects Laertes's "fair hour" (1.2.62) to include "drabbing" (2.1.26), indulgently blessing his son's right to "such wanton, wild, and usual slips / As are companions noted and most known / To youth and liberty" (22–24). However, both father and son regard it as their duty to insist that Ophelia avoid the "savageness in unreclaimed blood, / Of general assault" (34–35). Polonius reduces her to confusion about Hamlet's "many tenders / Of his affection" (1.3.99–100)—"I do not know, my lord, what I should think" (104)—and extracts her obedience to his peremptory command to end her "free and bounteous" "audience" (93) with Hamlet—"I shall obey, my lord" (136). Polonius completes this manipulation of Ophelia by directing her to stage an audience designed to catch Hamlet's love: "I'll loose my daughter to him" (2.2.162). Yet though male control of a woman's destiny is a general problem in the society represented in this play, Hamlet manifests this problem with a personal vehemence indicative of his special situation.

For Hamlet, no independent view of Ophelia is possible because he can see her only as an extension of his agonized relation to his mother.[8] His alienation from Gertrude is already generalized in the outcry of his first soliloquy: "Frailty, thy name is woman!" (1.2.146). His attraction to Ophelia becomes automatically a casualty of this generalization. We hear of Hamlet's earlier poetic worship of her " 'excellent white bosom' " (2.2.113) only in retrospect: " 'To the celestial and my soul's idol, the most beautified Ophelia' " (110).

The moment when Polonius expects to trap Hamlet's "hot love" (2.2.132) is the moment when Hamlet renounces it, breaking the bond with Ophelia by his reiterated "Farewell" (3.1.132, 137, 140). His separation from Ophelia begins in self-accusation and ends in a misogynist outburst. His first sight of "The fair Ophelia" makes him conscious of "all my sins" (88–89). The failure of love is Hamlet's: "You should not have believ'd me, for virtue cannot so innoculate our old stock but we shall relish of it. I lov'd you not" (116–18). But Hamlet then turns his attention to the procreation that should be sanctified by marriage and proclaims an indiscriminate revulsion that embraces his mother, himself, and Ophelia, to whom he remonstrates: "Get thee to a. nunn'ry, why wouldst thou be a breeder of sinners? I am myself indifferent honest, but yet I could accuse me of such things that it were better my mother had not borne me" (120–23). Even as he tries to sever the bond with his mother, he asserts it, while transferring to Ophelia the image of the contaminating mother. Hamlet's need for purity drives him to shift quickly from male deception to female deception, his final diatribe emphatically placing responsibility on women: "You jig and amble, and you lisp, you nickname God's creatures and make your wantonness your ignorance" (144–46).

In a play in which the image of a good woman is not convincingly restored to the male imagination, it proves easier to find a good man. Hamlet's adoration of Ophelia is transferred to Horatio, whom Hamlet suddenly sees as his new soul's idol: "Since my dear soul was mistress of her choice / And could of men distinguish her election, / Sh' hath seal'd thee for herself" (3.2.63–65). In Hamlet's eyes, women are inherently two-faced: "God hath given you one face, and you make yourselves another" (3.1.143–44). In a world where love between men and women has become irrevocably duplicitous, sexuality can be avoided by turning to male ties to fashion a dependable bond. The stoic imperviousness of Horatio's relation to fortune—as " 'strumpet Fortune' " (2.2.493) the epitome of inconstant woman—has a purity that recommends him. By contrast, Hamlet con-

demns Rosencrantz and Guildenstern for living "in the se-
cret parts of Fortune" as "her privates" (2.2.235, 234).

The passionate transfer of trust to Horatio in act 3, scene
2, is underscored by Hamlet's treatment of Ophelia, which
immediately follows. Though he is still cruel, his sexual
antagonism during the play within a play has become a
settled routine. The decrease in the emotional intensity of
his misogynist rhetoric suggests that his detachment from
Ophelia has been completed. Once formulated, Hamlet's
severely disillusioned attitude toward women remains essentially constant. His fleeting recollection of his love after
Ophelia's death confirms that his ideal image of woman is
effectively beyond recovery. The brief assertion that "I
lov'd Ophelia" (5.1.269) is relatively weak in a scene that
gives the central emphasis to Hamlet's fraternal rivalry
with Laertes. Hamlet does attain a sense of equanimity in
the final act, but this positive spirit is carried primarily by
his interactions with Horatio and Laertes. The release from
the claustrophobic "nutshell" of Hamlet's misogynist "bad
dreams" (2.2.254–56) is never dramatized, and the disturbed attitude toward female sexuality is neither squarely
faced nor transformed and resolved.

This relationship between Hamlet and Horatio is reinforced by the parallel relationship between Hamlet and
Laertes. "By the image of my cause," Hamlet sees "the
portraiture of his" (5.2.77–78), though he might equally
well have noted the analogy between his situation and
Ophelia's. But it is Laertes rather than his sister who is
the primary focus of Hamlet's "tow'ring passion" (80).
Ophelia occasions the men's involvement with each
other: "I lov'd Ophelia. Forty thousand brothers / Could
not with all their quantity of love / Make up my sum.
What wilt thou do for her?" (5.1.269–71). The dramatic
force of this scene lies in the use of "quantity" and "sum"
rather than of "love," as Hamlet turns Laertes's display
into a competitive challenge that he can win. Hamlet's

scene with Laertes ends without reconciliation: his "I lov'd you ever" (290) goes unanswered. Yet their violent embrace in the grave is converted into brotherly alliance when the two absolve each other (without reference to Ophelia): "Exchange forgiveness with me, noble Hamlet. / Mine and my father's death come not upon thee, / Nor thine on me!" (5.2.329–31). Hamlet forgives Laertes, entrusts his story to Horatio, and even generously extends his "dying voice" (356) to Fortinbras. The redemptive spirit of the conclusion is thus created by Hamlet's enclosing himself in male fellowship, an envelopment to which we may critically respond: "Something too much of this."

Considering how much is destroyed and how much is left unresolved, it is remarkable the way the final scene insists on an afterlife for its hero. This positive dimension is not found in the ending of any other major tragedy until *Antony and Cleopatra*, where we do in part believe Cleopatra's "immortal longings" because they are counterbalanced by Octavius's reality, albeit "paltry." Yet Hamlet's "felicity" (5.2.347) cannot withstand the strict criterion of accountability evoked earlier by Claudius:

> but 'tis not so above:
> There is no shuffling, there the action lies
> In his true nature, and we ourselves compell'd,
> Even to the teeth and forehead of our faults,
> To give in evidence.
>
> (3.3.60–64)

The final scene protects Hamlet by suspending critical evaluation of his felicity and the fraternal commitment that supports it. We must feel the authentic emotional power of the Hamlet–Horatio bond yet also note the way it deflects Hamlet from his problematic relations with women and allows him to escape all responsibility for his part in those disastrous relations. Hamlet's use of the feminine soul in his declaration to Horatio (3.2.63–65) makes explicit the incorporation of the feminine into the male bond. As in the androgyny of *As You Like It*, there is a crucial distinction between a man's appreciation of the feminine and his devaluation of actual women. The force of this distinction suggests how the insularity of the Hamlet–Horatio bond can be both affecting and misogynist, the latter because of the unacknowledged way the formation of their bond depends on an abusive dismissal of Ophelia.

Hamlet and *Othello* are strikingly different. Where Hamlet is protected by the design of his play, Othello is exposed. In *Othello*, the male hero's view of women moves much more rigorously through three distinct phases: idealization, degradation, and belated return to the original idealization. Unlike Hamlet, Othello decisively recovers his initial perception of the good woman and is forced to confront his responsibility for her destruction. Moreover, *Othello* attacks the indulgent sentimentality surrounding male bonds by transforming the Hamlet–Horatio pair into the Othello–Iago bond. Othello's desperate transfer of trust from "that cunning whore of Venice / That married with Othello" (4.2.88–89) to the "honest" male companion is ruthlessly undercut.

II

Act 1 of *Othello* seems to unfold according to the comic formula of *A Midsummer Night's Dream*. Brabantio, like Egeus, is the stock type of the irate father whose defeat we welcome. But the mechanism that allows Othello to win Desdemona despite her father's opposition is not, as in *A Midsummer Night's Dream*, the "green world," but rather the authority of the male state. Othello's dramatic role is framed by reference to this state. His first words confidently assert the connection between himself and the state: "My services which I have done the signiory / Shall out-tongue his complaints" (1.2.18–19). His last words more ruefully reiterate this claim: "I have done the state

some service, and they know't" (5.2.339). Part of the complexity of Othello's situation is that, like Hamlet, he has
to deal with two father figures, not one. The first father,
Brabantio, is easily dismissed, but the state acts as a second, metaphorical father, with whom relations are more
difficult to control.

The very phrase "the state" has an impressive, impene-
trable ring in this play, and reference to it conveys self-evident, self-sufficient meaning that seems to make further
questions unnecessary. The entire action of the play is circumscribed by the presence of the state. It approves
Othello's marriage and sends him to Cyprus. We are kept
aware of it by Othello's allusion—"These letters give, Iago,
to the pilot, / And by him do my duties to the Senate"
(3.2.1–2)—and by Desdemona's assumption that Othello's
irritability comes from preoccupation with state business—
"Something sure of state" (3.4.140). Immediately after
Othello has reached the decision to murder Desdemona,
the state reenters in the person of its representative, Lodovico. Othello is now openly sardonic about the senators' authority: "I kiss the instrument of their pleasures" (4.1.218).
But though their orders unwittingly countermand Othello's
dismissal of Cassio in a way that Othello cannot help experi-
encing as a gratuitous rebuke, he still forces himself to submit to their command: "Sir, I obey the mandate, / And will
return to Venice.—Hence, avaunt! / Cassio shall have my
place" (259–61). Lodovico gives choric expression to the
state's shock at Othello's change: "Is this the noble Moor
whom our full Senate / Call all in all sufficient?" (264–65).
As the play's final lines indicate, ultimately the state is the
recipient of Othello's story: "Myself will straight aboard,
and to the state / This heavy act with heavy heart relate"
(5.2.370–71).

The role of the Senate is emphasized at the outset
when the first two scenes set up a political drama involv-
ing the collision of two self-confident men, whose resolution in scene 3 is the culmination of act 1. The source of

Brabantio's confidence is clearly specified at the conclusion of scene 2:

> The Duke himself,
> Or any of my brothers of the state,
> Cannot but feel this wrong as 'twere there own;
> For if such actions may have passage free,
> Bond-slaves and pagans shall our statesmen be.
> (95–99)

Brabantio's reliance on his position has already been dramatized in his threat to Roderigo in the opening scene: "My spirits and my place have in their power / To make this bitter to thee" (1.1.103–4). As Iago, who is equally conscious of his "place" (11) because he has failed to attain it, mockingly puts it: "You are a senator" (118). Exuding the security of the powerful, Brabantio feels that he can count on a sympathetic hearing from his fellow senators, so much so that he need not hide his racial prejudice because his "brothers of state" must share it. Othello's poise is all the more remarkable for his civility in the face of Brabantio's insulting disbelief that his daughter

> So opposite to marriage that she shunn'd
> The wealthy curled darlings of our nation,
> Would ever have, t' incur a general mock,
> Run from her guardage to the sooty bosom
> Of such a thing as thou—to fear, not to delight!
> (1.2.67–71)

Better Roderigo, whose suit Brabantio had earlier rejected (1.1.95–98), than a nonwhite "thing": "O would you had had her! " (175).

But Othello is immune not only to Brabantio's insistent provocation but also to Iago's. Othello's imperturbable self-assurance rests on his sense of place, his version of alliance with the state. His previous service has already manifested "my parts, my title, and my perfect soul" (1.2.31), and so will further service. He commands the scene with Brabantio by coolly appealing to a higher authority: "How may the Duke be therewith satisfied, / Whose messengers are here about my side, / Upon some present business of the state" (88–90). The Venetian council must choose between two vested interests: the instinctive tendency to support Brabantio as a fellow senator and the overriding issue of military defense in the Cyprus wars, for which Othello is indispensable. The priority of the latter emerges in scene 3 when the Duke of Venice turns immediately to the business underscored by the epithet accorded to Othello: "Valiant Othello, we must straight employ you" (1.3.48). Brabantio is almost lost in the shuffle: "I did not see you" (50). The outcome of the conflict between Brabantio's "particular grief" and "the general care" (54–55) is already clear, Iago having rehearsed it in advance (1.1.147–53; 1.2.11–17). The way in which the Senate's decision-making is dramatized and the way in which Othello positions himself in relation to the state are crucial. The dramatic structure enacts the social structure.

Initially the duke upholds Brabantio's expectations:

> Who e'er he be that in this foul proceeding
> Hath thus beguil'd your daughter of herself,
> And you of her, the bloody book of law
> You shall yourself read in the bitter letter
> After your own sense; yea, though our own proper
>   son
> Stood in your action.
>
> (1.3.65–70)

Not only does the duke act without information, he licenses Brabantio to use "law" as an instrument of personal revenge, a "bloody book" whose "bitter letter" Brabantio should interpret "after your own sense." Only after learning that "Who e'er he be" is the urgently needed Othello, who under the circumstances is in effect "our own proper son," does the duke slide away from this unrestrained commitment. Part of the drama involves our seeing the duke's about-face. The shift is registered in

the duke's adoption of a more critical approach to Brabantio's accusation: "To vouch this is no proof" (106). The
need to believe Othello's account is so strong that the
duke is convinced even before he hears corroborating evidence from Desdemona: "I think this tale would win my
daughter too. / Good Brabantio, / Take up this mangled
matter at the best" (171–73). Before the scene ends with
the conclusion of the unfinished state business, Brabantio
is allowed to respond to the duke's "sentence" (199)
about "patience" (207), the "patience" (4.2.63) against
which Othello's suffering will later bristle. Here Brabantio's "words are words" (1.3.218) creates a pause that
momentarily exposes the duke, whose action in support-
ing Othello over Brabantio is partly a matter of political
expediency that is poorly concealed by stoic saws.

Othello's magnificent verbal performance is essential in
enabling the Senate's declaration of self-interest in the
Turkish crisis to proceed smoothly. He retells the Senate
"the story of my life" (1.3.129) that he had earlier told to
woo Desdemona. "Out-tongue" (1.2.19), his term for the
competition with Brabantio, proves apt, for Othello's
sense of his life as a story is matched by his ability to tell
it, leisurely to "run it through" (1.3.132). Othello pours
into the state's ear a story the senators, like Desdemona,
are hungry to hear, appreciate, and confirm. His story is
irresistible: ironically the father who now objects to its
"witchcraft" (169) is its original "prompter" (1.2.84): "Her
father lov'd me, oft invited me; / Still question'd me the
story of my life" (1.3.128–29). Othello's elopement places
him in a situation where once again he "draws," this time
from the Senate, "a prayer of earnest heart / That I would
all my pilgrimage dilate" (152–53), and then he agrees to
the request he has elicited: "I did consent" (155). This
convolution in the relations between teller and listener
signifies Othello's special provision for the latter's collaboration. He rearranges the usual roles of active and passive
to make the listener's part far more active, as Desde-

mona's "greedy" and "devouring" ear (149–50) suggests. In the very process of telling the story, the teller re-creates and courts the danger he has faced as an adventurer: "And of the cannibals that each other eat" (143).

Othello's rhetoric insists on mutual dependence with the Senate, his present audience. His elaborate deference goes beyond the requirements of politeness and protocol. Nor is this deference simply a calculated play on his literal dependence: "The trust, the office I do hold of you, / Not only take away, but let your sentence / Even fall upon my life" (1.3.118–20). Othello's opening apology bespeaks a genuine need to disclaim his oratorical powers:

> Rude am I in my speech,
> And little bless'd with the soft phrase of peace. . . .
> And therefore little shall I grace my cause
> In speaking for myself. Yet (by your gracious patience)
> I will a round unvarnish'd tale deliver.
>
> (81–82, 88–90)

From his own perspective, Iago mocks this linguistic self-consciousness as "bumbast circumstance" (1.1.13). But the contradiction between Othello's sense of verbal inadequacy and his spectacular verbal success goes deeper than *sprezzatura*. His mode of address to the senators institutes a defensiveness he seems actually to feel:

> Most potent, grave, and reverend signiors,
> My very noble and approv'd good masters.
>
> (1.3.76–77)

> And, till she come, as truly as to heaven
> I do confess the vices of my blood,
> So justly to your grave ears I'll present.
>
> (122–24)

> Most humbly therefore bending to your state.
>
> (235)

Despite his clear-cut triumph over Brabantio, we feel that Othello's position is precarious, and not only because of the misplaced trust with which he turns to Iago (283–85). This vulnerability stems in part from Othello's social situation. The case of Hamlet provides a useful comparison. As son and heir to the king, Hamlet had been at the center of power. The murder of his father and Hamlet's consequent dispossession transform him into an alienated outsider and push him to the periphery of Claudius's court, the sidelong position from which he launches his asides when we first see him in act 1, scene 2. Othello moves in the opposite direction. He is an outsider who has made his way into the Venetian power structure. With the acceptance of his marriage to Desdemona, he reaches the center of Venetian society and consolidates his place within it. His phrase "to as proud a fortune / As this that I have reach'd" (1.2.23–24) speaks to this experience of advancement. Nevertheless, as act 1, scene 3, so dramatically shows, his position remains unstable because it is based on the state's ulterior need for Othello's military ability.

Furthermore, Othello's military vocation keeps him at the margins of the society. He serves Venice at the borderline between "civilization" and "barbarism." Himself an outsider on the inside, he protects Venice from outsiders.[9] The difficulty in maintaining this identity shows in Othello's consternation at the disruption on Cyprus: "Are we turned Turks, and to ourselves do that / Which heaven hath forbid the Ottomites?" (2.3.170–71). At the end of the play, Othello crosses back over the line and imagines part of himself as "a malignant and a turban'd Turk" (5.2.353) in order to kill himself. His self-image is destroyed when he himself is pulled into the category of a non-Christian alien against whom he had been commissioned to defend Venice. And this tragic culmination originates in the initial paradox that although Venice needs Othello to defend its purity from foreign barbarism, he is also a source of impurity as defined by Brabantio's unabashed exhibition of racial prejudice.[10]

The pressure on Othello's identity is increased at the point when the play shifts from urban Venice to the outpost at Cyprus, "this warlike isle" (2.1.43). In the dispute with Brabantio, Othello could appeal to the Senate whereas on Cyprus there is no higher authority who can mediate the conflict: Othello must take charge himself. This transition is emphasized by Montano's praise of Othello's leadership (30, 35–36). But his leadership begins to fail as soon as he confronts his first crisis: "My blood begins my safer guides to rule, / And passion, having my best judgment collied, / Assays to lead the way" (2.3.205–7). The metaphorical application of his individual chaos to the political realm is clear here as it is later in Othello's brittle assurance to Iago: "Fear not my government" (3.3.256). As the absence of the state contributes to Othello's disintegration, so its presence facilitates his self-control, a control Othello vows to keep in his last long speech to the duke before departing for Cyprus:

> And heaven defend your good souls, that you think
> I will your serious and great business scant
> For she is with me. No, when light-wing'd toys
> Of feather'd Cupid seel with wanton dullness
> My speculative and offic'd instruments,
> That my disports corrupt and taint my business,
> Let housewives make a skillet of my helm,
> And all indign and base adversities
> Make head against my estimation!
>
> (1.3.266–74)

This speech reflects the confessional relationship Othello feels he has established with the state: reassurance of the senators and reassurance of himself combine in a circular, mutually validating process. Along with this audience, Othello loses the protection it affords him when he moves to Cyprus.

Othello makes this self-defense in support of Desdemona's request to accompany him, after he had with "prompt alacrity" (1.3.232) agreed "to slubber the gloss" of his wedding and to go alone on the "more stubborn and boist'rous expedition" (226–28) assigned by the duke. But Othello's revised stance continues the firm separation of war and love, making his "estimation" hinge on this separation. Even if it is a danger that he can sweep aside as one that poses no threat to him personally, Othello does feel called upon to address the possibility "That my disports corrupt and taint my business" (271), and this declaration has the unfortunate side effect of demeaning love. He is "to be free and bounteous to her mind" (265), not her body, and thereby he reduces sexuality to the negative image of incapacitation and emasculation. In so sharply sorting out his priorities and asserting his manhood, Othello raises a doubt, however small, and tempts the fate—"Let housewives make a skillet of my helm" (272)—he later receives when "Othello's occupation's gone" (3.3.357).[11]

Circumstances abruptly deprive Othello of his military occupation, the basis of his preferred self-definition (1.3.229–34). Like Brabantio, the Turkish fleet is an external adversary that all too readily vanishes. The war for which there has been such a build-up is over before it begins because the tempest magically eliminates the enemy (2.1.20), as Othello himself announces:

> News, friends: our wars are done; the Turks are
> drown'd.
> How does my old acquaintance of this isle?
> Honey, you shall be well desir'd in Cyprus,
> I have found great love amongst them. O my sweet,
> I prattle out of fashion, and I dote
> In mine own comforts.
>
> (202–7)

We can hear a slight giddiness, as well as the pleasurable anticipation of sexual "fruits" (2.3.9), in his voice as he makes the decisive shift from war to love, turning to the "disports" (1.3.171) he had earlier dismissed in favor of the Senate's "serious and great business" (267). Just as before the private story of Othello's wooing is made public property through his account of it to the senators, so now the whole society is invited to participate in the wedding festivity:

> It is Othello's pleasure, our noble and valiant general, that . . . every man put himself into triumph; some to dance, some to make bonfires, each man to what sport and revels his addiction leads him; for besides these beneficial news, it is the celebration of his nuptial.
>
> (2.2.1–7)

Othello's careful instruction to Cassio—"Let's teach ourselves that honorable stop, / Not to outsport discretion" (2.3.2–3)—is insufficient to check the festive release of "addiction" called forth by public proclamation.

Act 2, scene 1, presents three images of Desdemona.[12] The third image—Othello's emotional response—is delayed until his arrival; in the meantime, the first two versions contrast sharply. Cassio's sublime "divine Desdemona" (73) seems incompatible with Iago's ridiculous housewife who "suckles fools and chronicles small beer" (160)—Iago's answer to Desdemona's idle question: "What wouldst write of me, if thou shouldst praise me?" (117). Incapable of fulfilling her request to celebrate "a deserving woman indeed" (145) since for him good women do not exist, Iago instead applies his poetic "invention" (125), his "Muse" (127), to satirical deflation. The result makes women "lame and impotent" (161), as Desdemona rightly protests. Cassio's appeal to poetry is diametrically opposed, emphasizing the woman's power rather than male wit. The exalted lady is portrayed as so overpowering that she exhausts poetic invention:

> he hath achiev'd a maid
> That paragons description and wild fame;
> One that excels the quirks of blazoning pens,
> And in th' essential vesture of creation
> Does tire the ingener.
>
> (61–65)

This image of perpetual exhaustion carries over to the lovemaking that Cassio compresses into a single line: "Make love's quick pants in Desdemona's arms" (80).

The social benefits overflowing from this sexual act are great. But so are the risks. Othello approaches his goddess-wife armed with Jove's superhuman force and a heroic erection ("his tall ship"), while the consummation is a propitiatory ritual performed before a powerful woman whose enfolding arms signify her control:

> Great Jove, Othello guard,
> And swell his sail with thine own pow'rful breath,
> That he may bless this bay with his tall ship,
> Make love's quick pants in Desdemona's arms,
> Give renew'd fire to our extincted spirits,
> And bring all Cyprus comfort!
>
> (2.1.77–82)

The impression of female control is simply stated at the beginning of the speech in Cassio's allusion to "our great captain's captain" (74). Othello himself—giving us the third image of Desdemona—acknowledges her power by his startling greeting, "O my fair warrior!" (182). Why does Othello accord her this epithet of war?

In its romantic dimension, *Othello* draws on the potential conflict between two elements in chivalric culture: devotion to heroic deeds and devotion to the lady who inspires them. The former suggests the male hero's "unhoused free condition" (1.2.26) whereas the latter suggests subordination to a higher female power. The narrative Othello tells the Senate in act 1, scene 3, presents these two elements in sequence as his heroic achievements are first won, then given over to the woman he serves. As his account makes clear, he literally transfers his warrior identity to Desdemona through the storytelling that constituted his courtship. Because of her ideal response (1.3.158–61, 167–68), Othello makes Desdemona the repository and guardian of his story. She thereby becomes the "fair warrior" to such a degree that (apparent) loss of Desdemona's love automatically entails loss of his heroic vocation: "Othello's occupation's gone" (3.3.357). His extreme vulnerability can be counteracted only by an equally extreme resort to the violence that had formerly served him so well in the military sphere, and Iago, with his instinct for weakness, knows how to manipulate Othello's dedication to Desdemona by parodying it (2.3.345–48).

In the convention of courtly love, the feudal relationship of lord and vassal is metaphorically applied to the fealty a man owes his beloved so that—in what amounts to a gender-role reversal—the woman becomes the man's lord and he her vassal. As Rosalie Colie has emphasized, this play "unmetaphors" poetic conceits by pushing them dramatically to their logical extreme.[13] Desdemona does not passively accept the power Othello attributes to her but actively seizes it. His romantic story is for her an erotic object that gives her "greedy ear" (1.3.149) a pleasure she eagerly "devours" (150). Nor is her goal simply sexual. Through Othello's story she gains access to a larger world beyond the domestic realm that presently confines her: "But still the house affairs would draw her thence, / Which ever as she could with haste dispatch, / She'ld come again" (147–49). Her determination to escape this realm is indicated first by her "challenge" (188) to her father, then by her implicit challenge to Othello as she sues the duke for permission to join Othello's expedition: "That I did love the Moor to live with him, / My downright violence, and storm of fortunes, / May trumpet to the world" (248–50). Her very language communicates her assimilation of Othello's story.[14] "The rites for why I love him" (257) include her consecration "to his honors" (254) and hence her participation in future chapters of the story she has heard. Othello does his best to keep her from the affairs of men:

OTH. Look if my gentle love be not rais'd up!
I'll make thee an example.
DES. What is the matter, dear?
OTH.   All's well now, sweeting;
Come away to bed. . . .
Come, Desdemona, 'tis the soldiers' life
To have their balmy slumbers wak'd with strife.
                    (2.3.250–54, 257–58)

Ultimately, only Emilia gives brief, tragic fulfillment to female transcendence of the domestic role: "Perchance, Iago, I will ne'er go home" (5.2.197).

Though kept within the bounds of her role as gracious wife, Desdemona's power is nevertheless sufficient to incite Othello's insecurity once he begins to doubt, as he does here:

                         'Tis not to make me jealous
To say my wife is fair, feeds well, loves company,
Is free of speech, sings, plays, and dances well;
Where virtue is, these are more virtuous.
                    (3.3.183–86)

Othello elaborates his ideal vision of Desdemona as wife even as he decides to murder her, so much so that Iago is hard-pressed to get Othello back on the track of revenge:

OTH. O, the world hath not a sweeter creature! She might lie by an emperor's side and command him tasks.
IAGO. Nay, that's not your way.
OTH. Hang her, I do but say what she is. So delicate with her needle! an admirable musician! O, she will sing the savageness out of a bear. Of so high and plenteous wit and invention!
IAGO. She's the worse for all this.
OTH. O, a thousand, a thousand times. And then of so gentle a condition!
IAGO. Ay, too gentle.
OTH. Nay, that's certain. But yet the pity of it, Iago! O Iago, the pity of it, Iago!
                    (4.1.183–96)

This is altogether too much pity to suit Iago's purposes, but the feelings that Iago is at pains to suppress reveal the nature of Othello's investment in Desdemona. The majestic vision of male power subserving female power—"She might lie by an emperor's side and command him tasks"—is Othello's way, despite Iago's denial. At the same time, she is still only an accomplished housewife, one whose singing is no match for male "savageness."

What prevents us from turning away in total disgust from Othello's excruciating delusion of his wife's unfaithfulness is his inability to maintain his self-righteous poses. Periodically, he breaks down and we are able to see what he suffers underneath the aggressive posturing. When he focuses on Desdemona, his hackneyed rejoinder to her plain question merely throws it back at her in an all-but-unbearable tirade of "What committed?" (4.2.70–81). Yet when he momentarily focuses on himself, he gives poignant expression to his suffering. His long speech (47–64) attempts a new summary of the story of Othello's life, now revised to take into account the events since his marriage to Desdemona. In particular, he has discovered the one kind of suffering he can neither surmount nor withstand: "The fountain from the which my current runs / Or else dries up: to be discarded thence!" (59–60). His ideal image of his relation to Desdemona is presented as painfully lost, giving extraordinary testimony to his view of her power as the unique "fountain" from which he receives life-giving "current."[15]

This view of the power relations between men and women is one Othello derives from the story his mother told him. Contrary to his denial in act 1 of the use of magic, his first gift to Desdemona—the handkerchief—is a kind of charm. According to Othello's magical thinking, it represents his original image of Desdemona that is now endangered by her suspected contamination:

> That handkerchief
> Did an Egyptian to my mother give;
> She was a charmer, and could almost read
> The thoughts of people. She told her, while she kept it,

'Twould make her amiable and subdue my father
Entirely to her love; but if she lost it,
Or made a gift of it, my father's eye
Should hold her loathed, and his spirits should hunt
After new fancies. She, dying, gave it me,
And bid me, when my fate would have me wiv'd,
To give it her. I did so.

(3.4.55–65)

Under ideal conditions, Othello's mother is able to "subdue my father / Entirely to her love." Similarly, Othello expects to be subdued entirely by the love of Desdemona, his "fair warrior." Since Desdemona uses the same verb to describe her love for Othello—"My heart's subdu'd / Even to the very quality of my lord" (1.3.250–51), their harmonious merging ought to be reciprocal. But the action of the play denies this mutuality. Instead, the central focus is on the lopsided symbiotic unity created by Othello's casting Desdemona in the cherishing maternal role and himself in the subordinate position of near-total dependence on her nurturant power.

The love figured in the handkerchief is marked by a precarious balance of power. The handkerchief contains within it a fatalistic curse on the ideal love it ostensibly celebrates, a curse pronounced by the final three lines of Othello's description: "The worms were hallowed that did breed the silk, / And it was dy'd in mummy which the skillful / Conserv'd of maidens' hearts" (3.4.73–75). The sacred quality of female chastity, which alone justifies Othello's submission to Desdemona, is linked in advance with death. Desdemona, like the "sibyl" (70), is given the power to have and to be the sacred icon, but she lives implicitly under the sign of the maidens whose "hearts" supplied the "mummy" in which the handkerchief is embalmed. The handkerchief converts readily in Othello's mind from love token to dire threat because the violence embedded in it makes an either/or proposition. So long as Desdemona is perceived to be faithful, male aggression is disarmed, diverted, and woven into the "web" whose magic is underwritten by sacrificial virgins. But once Othello believes Desdemona has violated her side of the bargain, the handkerchief licenses him to reassert his aggression and to mobilize the "prophetic fury" (72) of the connection between the maidens and his wife. He feels fully justified in killing Desdemona in order to ensure her purity: "Yet she must die, else she'll betray more men" (5.2.6). Having acted out the handkerchief's association of female chastity with dead maidens, Othello makes this equation over her lifeless body: "Cold, cold, my girl! / Even like thy chastity" (275–76). The logic of the handkerchief entitles Othello to "hunt / After new fancies" (3.4.62–63), but he restricts himself to a monogamous revenge in which a bloodless murder enables him to preserve her chaste image despite depriving her of life.

Othello's fantasy is not simply that Desdemona has betrayed him but rather that she has been unfaithful specifically with his best friend. Othello's apparent situation is roughly analogous to the poet's position in sonnets 40–42, with the major difference that while the poet tries to "excuse" (42.5), Othello's desperation takes the form of violent anger. His rage is all the more extreme because, unlike the isolated poet, Othello has Iago's encouragement to channel his feelings into action designed to recapture his masculinity, as Iago's goading prompts: "Would you would bear your fortune like a man!" (4.1.61), "Good sir, be a man" (65), "A passion most unsuiting such a man" (77), and "Marry, patience, / Or I shall say y' are all in all in spleen, / And nothing of a man" (87–89). As soon as "Othello's occupation's gone" (3.3.357), he discovers, with Iago's assistance, a new occupation of revenge and rises to heroic language to claim it (453–62).

Iago, who felt himself spurned by Othello—"I, of whom his eyes had seen the proof" (1.1.28)—fashions a fictional "ocular proof" (3.3.360) in order to secure his rightful position. He "serves his turn upon" Othello (1.1.42) at the moment when Othello, "greeting thy love" (3.3.469), accepts Iago's claim to be "your own for ever" (480). Iago's role is threefold: he helps to undermine Othello's marriage, he "displants" Cassio (2.1.276), and he provides in his own person an exclusive male bond that Othello can use to replace the two relationships he has lost. Initially, male friendship and marital love are portrayed as not only compatible but positively harmonious. Cassio has accompanied Othello in his wooing of Desdemona (3.3.70–73), a companionship that none of the three feels marriage must end. Othello's appointment of Cassio as his lieutenant ensures the continuation of their relationship, one that Desdemona believes does not threaten her. So secure is her confidence in the marital bond that she works to reinstate Cassio in her husband's good graces as "one that truly loves you" (48).

Othello's affection for Cassio is briefly but vividly implied at the moment he lets it go. Following Iago's account of male friendship mysteriously transformed from "terms like bride and groom / Devesting them for bed" to "opposition bloody" (2.3.180–81, 184) because "men are men" (241), Othello's exasperation is primed to disown the person who "frights the isle," including the newlyweds, "from her propriety" (175–76): "And he that is approv'd in this offense, / Though he had twinn'd with me, both at a birth, / Shall lose me" (211–13). This severance of brothers can be heard in Othello's terse, pained dismissal: "Cassio, I love thee, / But never more be officer of mine" (248–49). The transformation of Cassio from friend into rival is completed by the story of his love for Desdemona with which Iago "abuses Othello's ear" (1.3.395) and by the Senate's "deputing Cassio in his government" (4.1.237): "Cassio shall have my place" (261), announces the distraught Othello.

The final stimulus by which Iago prods Othello to manly revenge is the superimposed images of heterosexual and homosexual lovemaking:

> And then, sir, would he gripe and wring my hand;
> Cry, "O sweet creature!" then kiss me hard,
> As if he pluck'd up kisses by the roots
> That grew upon my lips; then laid his leg
> Over my thigh, and sigh'd and kiss'd.
>
> (3.3.421–25)

The double horror of this "dream" (427) sends Othello recoiling directly into his absolute commitment to revenge. Cassio's feverish talking in his sleep refers to his supposed love for Desdemona, but the immediate visceral impact of Iago's fabrication comes from the image, however fleeting, of Cassio's loving Iago. In contrast to this disturbing male contact, Iago offers himself as a chaste bride who joins Othello in "the due reverence of a sacred vow" (461) and in the ritual kneeling that guarantees his pledge. In losing Desdemona and Cassio, Othello thus appears to gain not only the purification of revenge but also the pure bond with Iago, whom Othello loves "not wisely but too well." Iago overturns Cassio's "daily beauty . . . That makes me ugly" (5.1.19–20) by insidiously casting himself in the image of male constancy expressed in sonnet 20: "A woman's gentle heart but not acquainted / With shifting change as is false women's fashion; / An eye more bright than theirs, less false in rolling" (3–5). Othello kills Desdemona only after he has definitive proof of Iago's constancy: "The voice of Cassio! Iago keeps his word. . . . / O brave Iago, honest and just, / That hast such noble sense of thy friend's wrong! / Thou teachest me" (5.1.28, 31–33).

The elimination of Desdemona and the exposure of Iago mean that Othello becomes guardian of his own story again. He must try to provide for himself the "pity" (1.3.161, 168) he had received from Desdemona. Much of the play's conclusion concerns Othello's efforts to reformulate his identity. The awareness that his story needs to be revised competes with the nostalgic impulse to preserve the story as he originally entrusted it to Desdemona during their courtship:

> I have seen the day
> That with this little arm, and this good sword
> I have made my way through more impediments
> Than twenty times your stop. But (O vain boast!)
> Who can control his fate? 'tis not so now.
>
> (5.2.261–65)

The break in the speech—"But (O vain boast!)"—marks Othello's agonized recognition of the discontinuity between his past and his present. Talking about himself in the third person implies that he sees himself from the outside with detached, albeit wistful, alienation from his former self: "Man but a rush against Othello's breast, / And he retires. Where should Othello go?" (270–71). He subsequently clarifies his use of the third person: "That's he that was Othello; here I am" (284). The verbs show the split between past and present. The contrast between "Othello" and "I" indicates that he renounces his right to his name, that he is no longer "Othello" in the heroic sense of the word.

In the second half of the final scene, Desdemona is gradually restored in Othello's eyes to her earlier position. Having turned her from "the gentle Desdemona" (1.2.25) into "that cunning whore of Venice / That married with Othello" (4.2.88–89), he now sees her as an angelic being:

> When we shall meet at compt,
> This look of thine will hurl my soul from heaven,
> And fiends will snatch at it. . . .
> Whip me, ye devils,
> From the possession of this heavenly sight!
> Blow me about in winds! roast me in sulphur!
> Wash me in steep-down gulfs of liquid fire!
>
> (5.2.273–75, 277–80)

This vision, portraying Desdemona's elevation to heaven and Othello's demotion to the company of devils, recreates in more extreme form the hierarchical relationship he originally desired and temporarily inverted: either she's above me or she's below me but never quite on the same human level. Desdemona's "perfect soul manifests her rightly," as Othello's chagrin acknowledges. Her commitment to goodness—"his unkindness may defeat my life, / But never taint my love" (4.2.160–61)—triumphs but places her out of reach.[16] Othello's belated testimony to her power (5.2.273–80) strains, so great is the gap between them, toward a self-annihilation that anticipates his suicide. His melodramatic language (279–80), parodying his earlier endurance of heroic suffering as recounted to Desdemona, suggests an escape through punishment that would render him not only speechless ("O, O!" [282]), but unconscious, oblivious.

In one sense, collapse into emotional numbness is the only appropriate response Othello can make to the shock of realizing his delusion. But the weariness that pervades his various attempts to sum up and take stock makes them equivocal. He seems at first to relinquish honor altogether: "But why should honor outlive honesty? / Let it go all" (5.2.245–46). Yet the word receives a complex twist when Othello is asked to account for himself: "Why, any thing: / An honorable murderer, if you will; / For nought I did in hate, but all in honor" (293–95). The tonal mixture includes indifference, sarcastic self-exposure, and the beginnings of self-defense as he hopes for the inquirer's indulgence ("if you will") and tentatively deploys the rhythms of his final self-justificatory speech ("For nought I did in hate, but all in honor" anticipates the see-saw motion of "not wisely but too well"). The rhetorical structure of Othello's last long speech makes palpable his attempt to achieve a balanced self-image, to find through verbal rhythm a fulcrum that will enable him to reconcile the two competing versions of himself. The effort to unify his identity fails. The "bloody period" (357) of suicide that ends his speech implicitly admits that he finds his words inadequate to the task of tragic self-definition. Something more needs to be said, and hence the transition: "Set you down this, / And say besides" (351–52).

The center cannot hold. In the final lines leading to his suicide, Othello is both the heroic Othello and the evil cultural outsider:

> And say besides, that in Aleppo once,
> Where a malignant and a turban'd Turk
> Beat a Venetian and traduc'd the state,
> I took by th' throat the circumcised dog
> And smote him—thus.
>
> (5.2.352–56)

But the connection between the "good" and the "bad" Othello is thoroughly ambiguous. As the "malignant . . . Turk," Othello admits his unworthiness, turning against himself the aggression he has wrongly directed against his wife; but as the state's defender, he asks us to remember his heroic feats and dignity. In the latter case, his death will be restitution for Desdemona's by a process of cancellation; as we recall the original Othello, so we are the more readily inclined to forgive and forget the "tragic loading of this bed" (363) by turning back to an earlier, happier time.

Critical interpretation of *Othello* often divides spontaneously into two camps, depending on how one chooses to view Othello's final speech. But we can incorporate both approaches by seeing that the two views are dramatized in the text as a conflict between insight and evasion, between "speaking of me as I am" and "extenuating" (5.2.342). Othello has intimations of self-discovery, but they struggle against his powerful need for self-deception, the latter contaminating the former.

Acting as though self-deception were an ignoble theme—beneath the dignity of tragic decorum—critics sometimes claim self-knowledge as the essential feature of tragedy and then proceed to find in the tragic hero a decisive self-understanding that the text does not bear out. If self-knowledge is not present, in this view, then the play is not a tragedy and is only a disappointment. Yet T. S. Eliot's curt remark about Othello's "cheering himself up" should not be a red flag that prevents us from seeing Eliot's more useful and more moving observations: "I have never read a more terrible exposure of human weakness—of universal human weakness—than the last great speech of Othello."[17] The crucial addition of "universal" helps to answer the objection usually raised against Eliot that his critical view of Othello entails, a priori, an unfeeling detachment, a cynical irreverence. A lucid account of Othello's wavering self-awareness is not in and of itself cruel: we should not use it to make fun of Othello and to congratulate ourselves on our superiority. Sensitive, sympathetic involvement is still required: we recognize that "the human will to see things as they are not" is not limited to Othello.[18] The ending of *Othello* makes us realize that "Human kind cannot bear very much reality," as Eliot later emphasized. Critical attention to a character's gestures of avoidance is not incompatible with heartfelt engagement, and it is a misplaced, superficial compassion that neglects to explore the "reality" the tragic hero "cannot bear."

I am moved to horror as much as pity by the spirit of regret that overtakes Othello, but in engaging this horror I want to change the direction of Eliot's statement: "Humility is the most difficult of all virtues to achieve; nothing dies harder than the desire to think well of oneself." Eliot implicitly points to a religious proposition that human nature is so constituted as inherently to impede "the most difficult of all virtues,"[19] whereas I wish to emphasize Othello's specific social situation. There are two transactions being negotiated in the final scene: Othello's struggle to come to terms with his responsibility for Desdemona's death and his attempt to reestablish his connection to the state through its on-the-scene representative. The latter encircles the former and deflects attention from it. One reason why it is difficult to give Othello sympathy in the way he asks for it is the public atmosphere surrounding his final effort to set the record straight on the question of his identity. Hamlet shows a similar concern for the ultimate form his story will take, but this concern is made more plausible to us because it is expressed in the context of Hamlet's intimate relationship to Horatio. Hamlet does not try to justify himself but instead simply appeals to Horatio to become the witness to his story: "Report me and my cause aright / To the unsatisfied" (5.2.339–40). The report is indefinitely postponed, the judgment permanently suspended. Othello's more highly pressured dramatic situation requires him to persuade an impersonal audience—ultimately "the state" (5.2.339, 354) that he addresses in his last long speech. The state functions psychologically as a kind of superego whom Othello is drawn to satisfy by presenting himself in the most favorable way possible. In thus speaking for the public record, he does not entirely resist the temptation to gloss over the magnitude of his error. But Othello is not alone in this attempted mitigation of his tragedy, for the whole social system cooperates with him.

The concern about how to improvise Othello's new story is shared, for instance, by Lodovico, who asks: "O thou Othello, that was once so good, / Fall'n in the practice of a damned slave, / What shall be said to thee?" (5.2.291–93). This open question suggests genuine bafflement and uncertainty that are quickly closed by a narrow focus on the clear-cut case of the "damned slave." There is an unwillingness not only on Othello's part but also on the part of others to draw the appropriate critical conclusions about Othello's tragedy. There is a sustained effort to deflect criticism from Othello by scapegoating Iago and by placing all blame on him: "This is thy work," insists

Lodovico (364). The disproportionate emphasis on Iago's torture provides a release that distorts Othello's major contribution to the tragic outcome. The torture motif is sounded not only in Lodovico's closing speech (367–69) but also at two earlier points (305, 332–35). Shakespeare thus dramatizes the characters' desire for an easy resolution. The play raises difficult questions about the scope of evil that the characters try to get around by pretending that the evil can be confined to Iago, so isolated and excised.

But Iago's last word is silence. Despite threats—"Torments will ope your lips" (5.2.305)—he refuses "to pray" (304), to acquiesce in the scapegoat role dictated by an oversimplified morality play. He will not cooperate by conforming to the part in the pious tale that might largely exonerate Othello as the devil's unfortunate victim. The final speech by Lodovico makes us feel that the Venetian state will not be given a full, accurate account of the tragedy we have witnessed. Shakespeare's ending is designed to make us hear a more complete and "honest" version than Lodovico's will be. The drama of the final scene includes a collaboration (not a conscious conspiracy) between Othello and the male state in its stress on Iago's torture that distracts from Othello's torture of Desdemona. By contrast, the ending of *King Lear* resolutely keeps the focus on the destroyed heroine. But the pressures against Lear's self-awareness are so strong as to reverse his initial recognition in act 4, scene 7, that he has done Cordelia wrong, with the result that no story can be told except Lear's sensation of utter deprivation: "Look there, look there!" (5.3.312).

III

King Lear elaborates further the dramatic possibilities of the two extreme versions of women between which Othello shuttles. The opening scene makes clear that Lear himself is the major source of this splitting, for he initiates the contest that provokes the division into good and bad daughters. Though they respond differently to this provocation, all three daughters share the common purpose of protecting themselves against the father's total claim on them. Lear subsequently satisfies his need to make a total claim through the absolute, unquestioning loyalty and devotion of the disguised Kent. Frustrated by women, Lear "sets his rest" on the "kind nursery" of male bonding (1.1.123–24).

Although Gloucester's programmatic pessimism tells us that "friendship falls off, brothers divide" (1.2.106–7), his own actions provide strong contrary evidence. At the risk of his life, Gloucester makes the commitment to "relieve" Lear with "charity" (3.3.14, 16). This male "kindness" (3.6.5) specifically includes nurturance: "Yet have I ventured to come seek you out, / And bring you where both fire and food is ready" (3.4.152–53). When the two are reunited after Gloucester has lost his eyes for protecting Lear (3.7.56–58), their shared suffering exemplifies "bearing fellowship" (3.6.107). In a more positive sense than Goneril intended, "Old fools are babes again" (1.3.19), as Lear and Gloucester are now in a position to survey their existence from the perspective of birth: "we came crying hither. / Thou know'st, the first time that we smell the air / We wawl and cry" (4.6.178–80). For a brief but moving moment, the two men succor each other.

The comfort of male bonding is a powerful force in the play's final scene. Edgar recounts his reunion with Kent:

> With his strong arms
> He fastened on my neck and bellowed out
> As he'd burst heaven, threw him on my father,
> Told the most piteous tale of Lear and him
> That ever ear received.
>
> (5.3.212–16)

Edgar, who "by the art of known and feeling sorrows" has been made "pregnant to good pity" (4.6.222–23), also has a "most piteous tale" to tell about "nursing" Gloucester's "miseries" (5.3.181–82). Even Edmund is drawn into this circle of male sympathy when he is affected by his brother's narration: "This speech of yours hath mov'd me, / And shall perchance do good" (200–1). His otherwise implausible conversion—"Some good I mean to do, / Despite of mine own nature" (244–45)—is given cogency by his abandonment of the alliance with Goneril and Regan and his return to the all-male family. Edgar's brotherly gesture of "exchanging charity" (167) completes the process of male purification initiated by the rite of single combat whereas the source of evil is regarded as the female site of Edmund's begetting: "the dark and vicious place where thee he got" (173).

Edmund himself is separated from female contamination because the play treats the three conspicuously evil characters differentially by gender. Goneril and Regan engage in a comical and self-destructive competition for Edmund's body, striving to outdo each other in their haste to promise Edmund the obedience and solicitous care they deny Lear. The sex-role reversal with which Goneril taunts her husband's "milky gentleness" (1.4.341) dissolves when she succumbs to Edmund: "O, the difference of man and man! / To thee a woman's services are due" (4.2.26–27). Unlike Goneril and Regan, Edmund is not compromised by the ironies of their love triangle, which he is allowed to view with bemused detachment:

> To both these sisters have I sworn my love;
> Each jealous of the other, as the stung
> Are of the adder. Which of them shall I take?
> Both? one? or neither?
>
> (5.1.55–58)

Edmund's detachment from the women's love is enacted when he ignores Goneril's cue to dismiss the single combat with the disguised Edgar as "practice" (5.3.152). Edmund does not have to say "Shut your mouth, dame"

(155) because another male says it for him, but he willingly binds himself to the integrity of this male trial and its outcome. While Goneril stonewalls (161), Edmund imagines "forgiveness" for his "noble" rival (167, 166). Though he has represented the manhood inspired by "the lusty stealth of nature" (1.2.11), Edmund, like Lear, at last gains access to manly pity.

To counter his daughters' "unkindness" (3.2.16), Lear assembles a ragged band of brothers and fashions a male refuge on the exposed heath. Kent, the Fool, and Edgar are Lear's shadows, who try to tell him who he is (1.4.230–31). In Kent's version, Lear's authority rests on masculine firmness backed by the willingness to use force. Kent devotes himself to restoring Lear's "frame of nature" to "the fix'd place" of "manhood" (268, 269, 297). As Lear's surrogate, Kent displays the aggressiveness in which Lear himself has been deficient. Kent's aggression in the service of goodness is instantly recognized by Lear as "love" (88) and rewarded (94) when the disguised Kent trips up the "base football player" (86) Oswald, Goneril's steward. Kent again courts violence with the verbal and physical attack on Oswald (now "the son and heir of a mungril bitch" [2.2.22]) that lands him in the stocks. Kent's antagonism, which elicits the "violent outrage" "upon respect" (2.4.24) and forces Lear into acute awareness of his diminished power, is described by both sides as a product of blunt manliness: "put upon him such a deal of man" (2.2.120) and "having more man than wit about me" (2.4.42). This manhood carries an antifemale note, for Kent's lack of vulnerability to women is one of the qualities by which he recommends himself to Lear's service: "Not so young, sir, to love a woman for singing, nor so old to dote on her for any thing" (1.4.37–38).

In the Fool, Kent's aggressive action takes the form of aggressive wit. The Fool baits both Goneril ("the Lady Brach" [1.4.112]) and Lear to bring home the powerless-

ness Lear has brought upon himself by disordering the
traditional gender hierarchy. Relentlessly exposing Lear's
weakness the better to push him toward a renewal of
manhood, the Fool mocks Lear's sex. Having given "the
rod" (174) to his daughters, Lear's penis is "a sheal'd
peascod" (200), an empty symbol of masculine power that
makes him a woman: "now thou art an O without a
figure" (192–93).[20] The Fool's pointed humor has a misogynist edge: "For there was never yet fair woman but
she made mouths in a glass" (3.2.35–36). Edgar, the third
member of Lear's male chorus, picks up the antifeminist
line when he warns against "the act of darkness" (3.4.87):
"Let not the creaking of shoes nor the rustling of silks
betray thy poor heart to woman. Keep thy foot out of
brothels; thy hand out of plackets" (94–97). However,
while Kent and the Fool press their single-minded attempt to shore up Lear's masculinity, Edgar evokes in
Lear a more complicated response.

Lear's immediate identification with Edgar—"Didst thou
give all to thy daughters? And art thou come to this?"
(3.4.49–50)—can be explained in part as a projection that
reinforces tough-minded hostility toward women. But Edgar's status as a beggar implies vulnerability—his "presented nakedness" hopes to "enforce their charity" (2.3.11,
20)—as well as defiance. Edgar answers to the self-image of
beggar that Lear has already begun to adopt for himself:

> "On my knees I beg
> That you'll vouchsafe me raiment, bed, and food."
>   (2.4.155–56)

> Why, the hot-bloodied France, that dowerless took
> Our youngest born, I could as well be brought
> To knee his throne, and squire-like, pension beg
> To keep base life afoot. Return with her?
> Persuade me rather to be slave and sumpter
> To this detested groom.
>   (212–17)

> O, reason not the need! our basest beggars
> Are in the poorest thing superfluous.
>
> (264–65)

Once on the heath, Lear ceases to resist the beggar image and instead seeks it:

> Poor naked wretches, wheresoe'er you are,
> That bide the pelting of this pitiless storm,
> How shall your houseless heads and unfed sides,
> Your loop'd and window'd raggedness, defend you
> From seasons such as these?
>
> (3.4.28–32)

Lear's prayer (27) is answered by Edgar's voice calling from within the hovel and, shortly, by the actual presence of his "uncover'd body" (102), a physical state to which Lear exposes himself: "Thou art the thing itself: unaccommodated man is no more but such a poor, bare, fork'd animal as thou art. Off, off, you lendings! Come, unbutton here" (106–9). In his guise as beggar, Edgar performs a service for Lear, of which neither Kent nor the Fool was capable, by facilitating Lear's openness to vulnerability.

Nonetheless, this openly acknowledged vulnerability exacerbates the distrust of women. This moment in act 3, scene 4, can be too easily cited as evidence that Lear learns from his suffering according to the beneficent tragic view: "The art of our necessities is strange / And can make vild things precious" (3.2.70–71). But the newfound preciousness of "unaccommodated man" bespeaks a humanism that coexists with hatred of women, for Lear has two separate visions of the human body depending on whether "the thing itself" is male or female. One crux of the play lies in the juxtaposition of the "poor, bare, fork'd animal" that Edgar presents with the "simp'ring dame, / Whose face between her forks presages snow" (4.6.60–67) that Lear "anatomizes" (3.6.76) with all the sanctimony he can summon:

> But to the girdle do the gods inherit,
> Beneath is all the fiends': there's hell, there's
>   darkness,
> There is the sulphurous pit, burning, scalding,
> Stench, consumption.
>
>   (4.6.126–29)

Just as the Edgar who occasions Lear's humanist revelation becomes the "most learned justicer" (3.6.21) who helps Lear prosecute Goneril and Regan in the mock trial on the heath, so Lear uses the Gloucester who "sees feelingly" (4.6.149) as an ally in taking revenge against women. Lear's critique of justice—"Why dost thou lash that whore?" (161)—applies to his own rhetorical assault on the female body, but he is blissfully unaware of the self-application.

The "darkness" (4.6.127) of the vagina is synonymous with heterosexual intercourse: "the act of darkness" (3.4.87) is the woman's "dark and vicious place" (5.3.173). Displaced from the male body and projected exclusively onto the female, sexuality becomes female sexuality; "copulation" (4.6.114) becomes a province for which women, not men, are responsible. In this view, the normal superiority of civilization to nature is reversed, transposed into an opposition between male necessity and female "luxury" (117); and between Edgar's salutary nakedness and the bad daughters' "plighted cunning" (1.1.280), literally imaged in their extravagant clothes (2.4.267–70) or in the verbal flattery by which Regan's "most precious square of sense" (1.1.74) disguises her "sulphurous pit" (4.6.128). Male perturbation with sexuality is greater here than in *Othello* because the sexual act is bound up with procreation. However repulsive the image of "making the beast with two backs" (*Othello*, 1.1.116–17), however convulsed Othello is by the thought of Desdemona "topp'd" (3.3.396)—"It is not words that shakes me thus. Pish! Noses, ears, and lips" (4.1.41–42)—there is nothing in *Othello* so alienated as Lear's life-denying curse against Goneril.

Lear takes revenge in a direct attack on her powers of gestation. Into her "sulphurous pit," he would "convey sterility" (1.4.278). If he cannot make her infertile, he condemns her to reproduce the filial ingratitude she has inflicted on him: "Turn all her mother's pains and benefits / To laughter and contempt" (286–87). Lear's earlier curse against Cordelia also strikes against procreation: "Better thou / Hadst not been born than not t' have pleased me better" (1.1.233–34). Lear finds particularly galling the physical intimacy of the blood connection that makes parent and child one flesh: "But yet thou art my flesh, my blood, my daughter— / Or rather a disease that's in my flesh, / Which I must needs call mine" (2.4.221–23). He employs several stratagems to try to sever this indissoluble bond. First, he banishes and disinherits: "Here I disclaim all my paternal care" (1.1.113). Cordelia is now "my sometime daughter" (120), "Unfriended, new adopted to our hate, / Dower'd with our curse, and stranger'd with our oath" (203–4), "for we / Have no such daughter" (262–63).

Second, he attempts a mortification of the flesh, analogous to the self-mutilation proposed by Edgar—"Strike in their numb'd and mortified arms / Pins, wooden pricks, nails, sprigs of rosemary" (2.3.15–16). When Lear calls the storm down upon his head, he punishes his body in order to purify it while at the same time destroying the universal power of procreation that corrupted him: "Crack nature's moulds, all germains spill at once" (3.2.9). Ultimately, the separation of male spirit from female flesh is achieved by the death of the woman. The play comes to rest when the threat posed by the female body is ended: "Produce the bodies" (5.3.231), "seest thou this object?" (239). The potency of the "sulphurous pit" has been canceled, as the exhibition of silent bodies bears witness.

The motif of the missing mother is only a decoy, for the play's "darker purpose" produces mother figures to fill the vacuum left by the absence of Lear's wife.[21] He asks

for trouble by turning his daughters into mothers, as the
Fool indicates after the fact. Lear's divestment of his authority initiates the dismantling of patriarchal order and
the reinstatement of maternal power. A confusion in the
ideal of male beneficence emerges: Lear retains the self-
pitying image as "Your old kind father, whose frank heart
gave all" (3.4.20), when actually he had used giving all as
a means to receive all. He makes clear, in retrospect, the
terms of the bargain when he desperately appeals to
"tender-hefted" Regan to show "The offices of nature,
bond of childhood, / Effects of courtesy, dues of grati-
tude" (2.4.178–79) by immediately reminding her of the
gift by which he purchased these dues: "Thy half o' th'
kingdom hast thou not forgot, / Wherein I thee endow'd"
(180–81). But more often Lear suppresses the logic that
connects "So kind a father" (1.5.32) to his desire for "kind
nursery" (1.1.124). In the candor prompted by extreme
disappointment, Lear admits that he was maneuvering
"to set my rest" (123) on Cordelia's care of him. Instead of
the maternal comfort he had sought, he inadvertently re-
creates the pain of maternal abandonment. When he renounces Cordelia after she has denied her undivided affection, Lear elevates his rage to the heroic proportions of
the "barbarous Scythian" (116) and the "dragon" (122).
But Lear's image of the angry, devouring father is preceded by his invocation of a dangerous goddess—"The
mysteries of Hecat and the night" (110)—who modulates
into the powerful mother whose victim is Lear.

Lear defends against this mother by standing on the
ceremony of manliness (2.4.276–78). But once he has en-
tered the open heath in a stormy night "wherein the cub-
drawn bear would crouch" (3.1.12), he gives in to the
all-consuming experience of his infantlike vulnerability.
This is the burden of Lear's beggar imagery: the infant's
needy dependence on a mother's care. Edgar as the embodiment of beggary evokes a whole range of feelings
associated with this dependence—from the fear of depri-

vation to the hope of survival. The "unfed sides" of "poor naked wretches" (3.4.30,28) whose destitution Lear commits himself to share refers in part to the basic necessity of maternal nurturance. Yet Lear short-circuits awareness by attempting to recover an image of benevolent paternal bounty:

> O, I have ta'en
> Too little care of this! Take physic, pomp,
> Expose thyself to feel what wretches feel,
> That thou mayst shake the superflux to them,
> And show the heavens more just.
>
> (32–36)

Patriarchal liberality that redistributes the superflux is not the appropriate "physic" for Lear's central problem; this fantasy of reparation by a reformed male authority cannot serve as a substitute for the absence of maternal generosity, the "kind nursery" to which Lear has pinned his "unburthen'd" self (1.1.41). Male bounty, independent of women, cannot be sustained.

The crucial importance of women for a sane social order is underscored by Lear's inability to release himself from misogynist rage. Only Cordelia's intervention provides him with the "sweetened imagination" he needs (4.6.131). Cordelia is the "daughter / Who redeems nature from the general curse / Which twain have brought her to" (205–7) because she is both maternal and virginal. The elimination from the play of her husband (4.3.1–6) ensures her exclusive devotion to Lear. Her "organs of increase" (1.4.279) are not at issue because, despite her maternal ambience, she is kept from association with literal child bearing. Upon her reentry to the play, she obliges Lear in the role of the good, comforting mother, to which he had originally assigned her. The maternal aspect of her rescue is implied by her image as "Our foster-nurse of nature" (4.4.12); this physic is hers to bestow, not the doctor's. Cordelia's reference to "our sustaining corn" (6) is linked metaphorically to the natural restorative power of her tears: "All blest secrets, / All you unpublish'd virtues of the earth, / Spring with my tears; be aidant and remediate / In the good man's distress" (15–18).

The image of a patriarchal "pomp" that makes restitution by "shaking" its "superflux" cannot hold a candle to Cordelia's maternal kindness, so necessary to Lear's restoration. However poignant the relations among Lear's company of supportive men, this male bonding is finally a minor resource compared with the unequivocal centrality of Cordelia for Lear—a centrality that dominates the play after her reappearance in act 4, scene 4. This is the significance of Lear's nonrecognition of Kent (5.3.279–95) and of his inattention to the Duke of Albany's scheme for patriarchal justice (297–305). Such consolations are irrelevant to Lear's desolation: Cordelia's death makes it impossible for him to "taste" her "cup" (303, 305). The gods do not exist who can revive the "miracle" of her life so as to "make them honors / Of men's impossibilities" (4.6.55, 73–74). In contrast to *Othello*, *King Lear* places greater structural emphasis on the final phase in which the male protagonist regains his perception of the woman's innocence. The dramatic potential is increased because Lear is permitted, as Othello is not, to reunite with her while she is still alive and to ask her forgiveness.

This is not to say that Lear's reconciliation with Cordelia is entirely positive; on the contrary, it is irredeemably tragic. The play cautions us against false optimism by undercutting Edgar's premature, sententious "The lamentable change is from the best, / The worst returns to laughter" (4.1.5–6). But Edgar's optimism is incurable; he thinks he can "cure despair" (4.6.33–34; 5.3.192) and returns "the worst" to laughter by means of an upbeat narrative closure: "Burst smilingly" (5.3.200). The main plot, however, defies Edgar's efforts to fashion a happy ending. In Lear's case, the comic rebirth prepared for him "closes the eye of anguish" (4.4.15) in a way that has negative as well as positive implications. Gloucester, misapprehending Lear's madness, desires it to escape his own "ingenious feeling" (4.6.280):

> Better I were distract,
> So should my thoughts be sever'd from my griefs,
> And woes by wrong imaginations lose
> The knowledge of themselves.
>
> (281–84)

But for Lear the reverse is more nearly true. His madness has shown the way to sharpened awareness; his "repose" (4.4.12) leads to some loss of this acute consciousness.

The correct identification of "good" and "bad" daughters is not enough because Lear proceeds to take advantage of Cordelia's goodness. In the reconciliation scene, Lear discovers that he is to "drink" not the "poison" of Cordelia's revenge as he had expected (4.7.71) but rather her unconditional mercy. Yet the play's final scene begins with Lear's transformation of the original moment of forgiveness into a commemorative routine: "We two alone will sing like birds i' th' cage; / When thou dost ask me blessing, I'll kneel down / And ask of thee forgiveness" (5.3.9–11). His momentary openness to human contact—"Be your tears wet? Yes, faith" (4.7.70)—is superseded by a withdrawal into the hollow posture of omnipotent fantasy, hollow because it denies not only Edgar's reality but also Cordelia's. Authentic communication between father and daughter has ceased. To Cordelia's gentle nudge "Shall we not see these daughters and these sisters?" (5.3.7), Lear can offer only flat resistance: "No, no, no, no!" (8). Cordelia is subsumed in the escapist vision Lear constructs for both of them; she is not consulted: her part is once again to "Love, and be silent" (1.1.62). This appropriation of Cordelia is not an act of love but a violation of it that echoes and repeats Lear's ritual of possessiveness in the opening scene.[22]

The sacrificial nature of Cordelia's role is explicit: "Upon such sacrifices, my Cordelia, / The gods themselves throw incense. Have I caught thee?" (5.3.20–21). Her compliance thus caught, verbal assent is unnecessary: Cordelia accepts her "plight" (1.1.101) by crying. But Lear insists that she stifle her tears as he lapses into the mode of vengeful defiance that blots self-awareness: "Wipe thine eyes; / The good-years shall devour them, flesh and fell, / Ere they shall make us weep! We'll see 'em starved first" (5.3.23–25). Having secured the maternal symbiosis of "kind nursery," Lear redirects the mother's punishments of "starving" and "devouring" against his enemies. Superficially, the tragic ending is the result of external evil forces now beyond Lear's control. Yet the tragedy cannot be made to hinge on the technicality of failing to save Cordelia in time (237–57). To give credence to the possibility of a last-minute rescue is to hold out too much melodramatic faith in a benign resolution and to avoid feeling the depth of the tragic horror. Lear's entrance with Cordelia dead in his arms answers directly to his own evocation of "sacrifices" at the beginning of the scene. Though we are moved by the agony of Lear's deprivation, we must nonetheless question the particular way in which he had expected her to "redeem all sorrows / That ever I have felt" (267–68), as his ready conversion of Cordelia's forgiveness into her sacrifice has just demonstrated. Lear recognizes his immense loss and his initial error, but he repeats the error and never fully understands his contribution to the tragic outcome nor acknowledges his responsibility.[23] He can win from one daughter a suspension of tragic causation—"No cause, no cause" (4.7.75). But another speaks the harsh truth: "The injuries that they themselves procure / Must be their schoolmasters" (2.4.303–4). The play's rigorous tragic logic insists on the necessity that Lear pay the price for the continuing self-evasion exemplified by the dream vision of imprisonment with Cordelia. Though Lear does not want to hear the lesson taught by the stern schoolmaster tragedy, we must.

IV

Seen from the perspective of an overview, the sequence of *Hamlet* through *Othello* to *King Lear* reveals a gradual shift. The power of male bonding is diminished. From its crucial position in *Hamlet*, it is relegated to a secondary role in *King Lear*. There is a corresponding increase in the attention focused on the male hero's bond with the woman. Three later tragedies, *Macbeth, Coriolanus,* and *Antony and Cleopatra*, continue this trend.[24] In all three cases, the woman—Lady Macbeth, Volumnia, Cleopatra—is primary for the male protagonist; relations with men are secondary. As is often noted, each of the male heroes in these three plays is in a crucial, pressured relationship with a threatening, maternal woman; and each man undergoes a crisis of gender identity that decisively affects his action in the political sphere.

What is striking about the three plays as a group is the insistence on the woman as a maternal figure: it is as though Shakespeare worked his way around, circling back to explore the problems posed by Gertrude's role that *Hamlet* had broached but evaded. This interest in woman as mother includes specific attention to the maternal breast. Despite differences, *Macbeth, Coriolanus,* and *Antony and Cleopatra* have in common an arresting, upsetting image of the violation of maternal nurturance. Lady Macbeth's evocation of violently disrupted breast feeding is well known (1.7.54–58), but her attempt to convert the "milk" in her "woman's breasts" to "gall" (1.5.47–48) has a resonance with the transformations of the breast enacted by Volumnia and Cleopatra. The former replaces milk with blood, symbol of the "valiantness" she asserts her son has "suck'st . . . from me" (3.2.129):

> The breasts of Hecuba,
> When she did suckle Hector, look'd not lovelier
> Than Hector's forehead when it spit forth blood
> At Grecian sword, contemning.
>
> (1.3.40–43)

Cleopatra, in organizing her final self-image, chooses to blend the process of lactation with poisoning: "Dost thou not see my baby at my breast, / That sucks the nurse asleep?" (5.2.309–10).

These three distorted images of the breast draw their power to dismay from the belief that, rightfully understood, suckling epitomizes "the milk of human kindness." The three women in these plays seem designed to confirm the suspicion that women cannot be trusted with their own nurturant powers, that women will not only betray men but betray them at the source. This motif of breast feeding, despite its literal physical emphasis, has a larger social significance, for disturbed images of maternal nurturance coincide with disturbances in the circulation of patriarchal bounty. The two can be connected by assuming that the former incites the latter. Hence, difficulties between individual men and women need to be examined in the context of a more general institutional problem that stems from the association of maternal nurturance with the body politic.[25] One measure of the chaos brought on by Macbeth's regime, for example, is its frustration of this association: "Alas, poor country, / Almost afraid to know itself! It cannot / Be call'd our mother, but our grave" (4.3.164–66).

In all three plays the system of rewards—by which loyalty is assured and patriarchal society is held together—has gone awry. Political stability depends on the public perception of an exchange in which the king receives the service of his subjects and then cancels his indebtedness by repayment sufficient to allow the king to retain unquestioned authority. But in *Macbeth* this balance is upset when Duncan insists on his inability to repay Macbeth for the service he has rendered in his spectacular defense of the kingdom:

> The sin of my ingratitude even now
> Was heavy on me. Thou art so far before,

> That swiftest wing of recompense is slow
> To overtake thee. Would thou hadst less deserv'd,
> That the proportion both of thanks and payment
> Might have been mine! Only I have left to say,
> More is thy due than more than all can pay.
>
> (1.4.15–21)

Duncan's excessive expression of inadequacy goes beyond polite disclaimer to the point of undermining his own position.[26] Praise is a form of political currency; by dispensing it, the leader asserts his control. Duncan's profuse statement of his powerlessness to meet Macbeth's success with a proportionate recompense subverts hierarchical order, creating a vacuum that invites Macbeth to take action. Unlike Duncan, Malcolm at the end of the play does not lay himself open but announces repayment in an assured, precisely calculated manner: "We shall not spend a large expense of time / Before we reckon with your several loves, / And make us even with you" (5.9.26–28).

A parallel disruption in the leadership structure occurs in *Coriolanus* because the hero's single-handed exploits are so great as to threaten the role of the nominal commander. We are alerted to the potential problem of a challenge to hierarchal authority in the opening scene: "But I do wonder / His insolence can brook to be commanded / Under Cominius" (1.1.261–63). Coriolanus takes charge of battle operations as though implicitly criticizing Cominius (1.6.45–66) whereas the latter readily assents to Coriolanus's plan: "Yet dare I never / Deny your asking" (64–65). Cominius's capacity to manage the hero is further tested by Coriolanus's subsequent resistance to the rewards that would signify his reintegration into the social structure. Two ceremonies of praise and reward—the first on the battlefield immediately after Coriolanus's success (1.9), the second a conspicuous repetition before the Roman Senate, which Coriolanus walks out on (2.2)—are needed to attack the "modesty" that would enable Coriolanus to "stand /

As if a man were author of himself, / And knew no other kin" (5.3.35–37). The function of honoring Coriolanus as a means of laying upon him the claims of kinship is signaled by the strenuousness of Cominius's effort:

> You shall not be
> The grave of your deserving; Rome must know
> The value of her own. 'Twere a concealment
> Worse than a theft, no less than a traducement,
> To hide your doings, and to silence that
> Which, to the spire and top of praises vouch'd,
> Would seem but modest.
>
> (1.9.19–25)

> Too modest are you;
> More cruel to your good report than grateful
> To us that give you truly. By your patience,
> If 'gainst yourself you be incens'd, we'll put you
> (Like one that means his proper harm) in manacles,
> Then reason safely with you.
>
> (53–58)

The depth of the struggle between Cominius and Coriolanus is intimated in the way honor metaphorically becomes "manacles" that constrict the hero and so bring him under social control. Coriolanus must be honored at all costs; if necessary, honor will be forced on him so that the society's indebtedness to him will not remain unpaid. Yet the result is inconclusive. As with Duncan, Cominius's continuing protests of the inability adequately to praise suggest the precariousness of Coriolanus's assimilation so that we are left in doubt whether the rhetoric of praise can ever offset Coriolanus's achievement: "The man I speak of cannot in the world / Be singly counterpois'd" (2.2.86–87).

Finally, in *Antony and Cleopatra* as well, the use of bounty to maintain masculine order fails to work smoothly. Antony eludes the conventional praise that the Romans want so desperately to give him. As in *Coriolanus*, the hero's name is the talisman by which society urges its control over the hero's identity and tries to elicit the desired behavior. But Antony defies the code to which his name had earlier lent its meaning. He can place himself outside the social structure because, unlike Coriolanus, Antony finds "a world elsewhere" (*Coriolanus*, 3.3.135)—a genuine alternative to Roman society. His rejection of the old world takes the form of entertaining its disintegration: "Let Rome in Tiber melt, and the wide arch / Of the rang'd empire fall!" (*Antony*, 1.1.33–34). Though this perfervid wish does not come true, Antony's challenge to the social structure is nonetheless substantial because his deliberate, extravagant mismanagement of bounty effectively mocks the parsimonious gift-giving employed by upholders of the patriarchal order such as Malcolm and Octavius.

In each of the three plays, oral imagery that originates with the mother–infant dyad is transposed to society at large. Lady Macbeth's imagined destruction of her feeding babe permeates the play as a whole. Duncan's dependence on Macbeth makes him a passive feeder at the Macbeths' castle: "And in his commendations I am fed; / It is a banquet to me" (1.4.55–56). The murder of surfeited Duncan murders "life's feast" itself (2.2.37) so that "the wine of life is drawn" (2.3.95). The Macbeths' second community feast fails because Macbeth cannot "give the cheer" as his wife urges: "To feed were best at home; / From thence, the sauce to meat is ceremony, / Meeting bare without it" (3.4.32–36). An unnamed lord generalizes the occasion, making oral distress a central metaphor for political corruption, when he hopes that "we may again / Give to our tables meat, . . . / Free from our feasts and banquets bloody knives" (3.6.33–35). In *Coriolanus*, Menenius's metaphor of the body politic equates social harmony with the digestive process, implicitly translating Volumnia's withholding maternal nourishment from her son into a larger version of social hunger. In *Antony and Cleopatra*, the feasting that celebrates false harmony (2.7) is quickly succeeded by hostility imaged as devouring: "Then, world, thou hast a pair of chaps—no more, / And throw between them all the food thou hast, / They'll grind th' one the other" (3.5.13–15). In these plays, the absence of benign maternal sustenance and the absence of benign patriarchal bounty can be correlated by assuming that they mirror each other and, more precisely, that the latter reflects the former. Benevolent patriarchy is modeled on (and hence depends upon) the domestic microcosm in which the mother lovingly feeds her infant; when this model is lost because of an upsurge of destructive maternal imagery, then it is frighteningly difficult to sustain a belief in the idealized, harmonious "ceremony" (*Macbeth*, 3.4.35) that fosters patriarchal order.

In *Macbeth* restoration of order is contingent on the conspicuous exclusion of women; recovery is carried out by Macduff, who is technically not "of woman born" (5.8.15–16), and Malcolm, who is "yet / Unknown to woman" (4.3.125–26). The severence of male from female is symbolized by the contrast between witch-haunted Scotland and the England of "pious Edward" (3.6.27), who fills the need for a father figure to replace Duncan. Like Duncan, Edward is a "most sainted king" (4.3.109); unlike Duncan, he is also strong, able to provide Malcolm not only a haven but also manly soldiers like Siward. As an alternative to the maternal destructiveness of Lady Macbeth, Edward presents a paternal figure who indubitably possesses "the natural touch" (4.2.9). As Lady Macbeth transforms the "smiling" babe (1.7.56) into a physical ruin too horrible to contemplate, Edward applies his "healing benediction" to those whose disfiguration was "pitiful to the eye" (4.3.156, 151). This masculine "grace" (3.6.27; 4.3.159) promotes an allegorical purity, for his ability to heal scrofula is worded as a moral conquest: " 'Tis call'd the evil: / A most miraculous work in this good king" (4.3.146–47). The morality play neatness of this account of the relations between good and evil is reinforced by the inapplicability of a medical cure to the hopelessly evil Lady Macbeth. But this battle of English and Scottish "physic" is capable of a different interpretation. The Macbeths' lack of "some sweet oblivious antidote" that could "Cleanse the stuff'd bosom of that perilous stuff / Which weighs upon the heart" (5.3.43–45) forces them to confront individual moral responsibility: "the patient / Must minister to himself" (45–46).[27] By contrast, Edward's healing powers symbolize an ethic that relies on external, magical solutions. Such magical thinking provides the basis for the play's ending, with its escapist belief in an entirely masculine social order.

Chapters 4 and 5 present a detailed analysis of the male/female dialectic in, respectively, *Antony and Cleopatra* and *The Winter's Tale*. Both plays are crucial because each attempts a resolution to the impasse in the relationship between men and women demonstrated in *Macbeth* and *Coriolanus*. Antony and Leontes strive to connect with the central female character in ways unavailable to Macbeth or Coriolanus. Each enacts a revised, expanded version of the "all that may become a man" (*Macbeth*, 1.7.46).

·4·

Identification with the Maternal
in *Antony and Cleopatra*

The form of *Antony and Cleopatra* depends, to an unusual degree, on a mixture of genres.[1] So prominent is the generic question that how critics weigh the various elements in the mix becomes a chief determinant of their overall interpretation of the play. When the twin dangers of veering too sharply toward either classic tragedy or late romance are avoided, the play threatens to turn into a hybrid "mongrel tragi-comedy" that falls between the two main generic categories and is classified as farcical satire in the vein of *Troilus and Cressida*—far more complex, but equally petty and disillusioned. Despite some affinities with Shakespeare's late romances, *Antony and Cleopatra* cannot be treated primarily as romance. But the play also cannot be approached as a conventional tragedy consistent with Shakespeare's previous use of tragic form. Instead, *Antony and Cleopatra* should be seen as a new, distinctly different kind of tragedy. The contrast and discontinuity between two types of tragedy—the first represented by the major tragedies from *Hamlet* through *Macbeth* and *Coriolanus*, the second by the unique instance of *Antony and Cleopatra*— need to be emphasized.

I

Antony's relationship to a woman differs from relationships of earlier tragic heroes. The play's title, with its emphasis on the couple rather than the single hero, alerts us to this shift.[2] Approaching *Antony and Cleopatra* by way

of the earlier tragedies helps suggest what is special about
Cleopatra as a female character. Seen in the context of the
tragic period, her "ambiguity" can be interpreted as Shakespeare's attempt to transcend the simple either/or duality
of "good" women and "bad" women that has been a
mainspring of tragic destructiveness. A characteristic
strategy by male protagonists to cope with anxiety about
women is to divide them into two rigid categories based
on a series of dichotomies: good/bad, superhuman (goddess or angel)/subhuman (whore or beast), compliant/as-
sertive. In this series, moral terms overlap with psychological ones. The good woman is reassuring whereas the
bad woman appears dangerous and threatening. But
Cleopatra resists the categorization of good or bad
woman. Vestiges of this dichotomy remain externally in
the contrast between Cleopatra and Octavia and inter-
nally in the conflicting images of Cleopatra as whore and
goddess. However, Cleopatra is not contained by this
framework; she contains it. Octavia is too minor and ineffectual a figure to create a compelling counterpoint
whereas Cleopatra's "infinite variety" implies a fusion of
qualities that does not lend itself to schematic splitting.
Cleopatra subsumes the two major lines of female characters hitherto developed separately. The first group includes Ophelia, Desdemona, and Cordelia and leads to
the daughters of the late romances, Marina, Perdita and
Miranda. The second group includes Gertrude, Goneril
and Regan, Lady Macbeth and Volumnia. Cleopatra cannot be forced to fit either of these two central types because she combines aspects of both the youthful, sacrificial, beneficent, redemptive type and the fully sexual,
threatening type. Although she is clearly a formidable
and even treacherous woman, she is nonetheless presented with a sympathy not accorded to the standard
domineering, destructive female. In the standard tragic
ending, the woman dies first while the male protagonist
is left to survey the damage for which he is in large part

responsible. One measure of Cleopatra's stature is the reversal of this pattern because the woman survives to mourn the man.[3] This striking reversal creates a different kind of tragic conclusion, one in which the relationship between the man and woman is not so utterly destroyed: something may be salvaged from the ruin, loss may be converted into partial gain.

From the vantage point of the *Sonnets*, Antony's involvement with Cleopatra can be seen as an attempt to reclaim the dark woman whom the poet of the *Sonnets* so consistently degraded. The poet's suspicion of betrayal by the union of the fair youth with the dark woman is recapitulated when Antony in defeat exclaims that he has been undone by Cleopatra's collaboration with Octavius: "To the young Roman boy she hath sold me, and I fall / Under this plot" (4.12.48-49). This outburst, however, is characteristically momentary. Shakespeare allows nothing to disrupt Antony's fundamental commitment to Cleopatra. The emotional dynamic of the *Sonnets* is reversed: contempt is now reserved primarily for the youth (Octavius) instead of the dark woman (Cleopatra). Because Shakespeare preserves Antony's allegiance to Cleopatra, the play is able to explore an unprecedented, sustained involvement with a woman who would ordinarily inspire hostility and fear.

Cleopatra resembles the woman of the *Sonnets* with her dark complexion. She is, in her words, "with Phoebus' amorous pinches black" (1.5.28). Like the dark woman, Cleopatra employs artifice to "make defect perfection" (2.2.231). The poet of the *Sonnets* complains about the spell cast by the woman's "defect" (149.11) or "insufficiency" (150.2) and by her "art's false borrow'd face" (127.6). Like the dark woman, Cleopatra is sexually mature and active. This erotic power is perceived as a capacious, engulfing liquid force. The poet of the *Sonnets* begs admittance to the lady by arguing that he should be one in the indistinguishable many:

> The sea, all water, yet receives rain still,
> And in abundance addeth to his store,
> So thou being rich in *Will* add to thy *Will*
> One will of mine to make thy large *Will* more.
>   (135.9-12)

All the poet's attempts to control the woman through irony fail because the irony cuts two ways. Any criticism of the woman automatically becomes self-criticism because the poet, like Antony, cannot break away from the relationship. The poet is tormented by a split between judgment (131.12) and passion. Clear sight is to no avail because of the helpless submission of "my dear doting heart" (131.3). The poet deliberately encourages the bad faith that will conceal his "death" for as long as possible:

> If I might teach thee wit, better it were,
> Though not to love, yet love, to tell me so,
> As testy sick men, when their deaths be near,
> No news but health from their physicians know;
>   (140.5-8)

The attempt at self-deception remains, however, bitterly transparent: "Therefore I lie with her, and she with me, / And in our faults by lies we flattered be" (138.13-14). Hence, in an alternate mode, the poet seeks to reveal and to hasten the loss of self, which is the logical conclusion of his entrapment:

> My love is as a fever, longing still
> For that which longer nurseth the disease,
> Feeding on that which doth preserve the ill,
> Th' uncertain sickly appetite to please.
> My reason, the physician to my love,
> Angry that his prescriptions are not kept,
> Hath left me, and I desperate now approve
> Desire is death, which physic did except.
>   (147.1-8)

All the various notes in the poet's approach to the dark woman have echoes in Antony's response to Cleopatra. Antony shares what the poet calls "my o'erpress'd defense" (139.8). He struggles with a similar conflict between attraction and repulsion; he too wallows in self-reproach; the imagery of "nursing" and "feeding" in sonnet 147 is central to Antony's physical bond to Cleopatra; his "desire" leads ultimately to "death" (147.8). Although the resemblances are substantial, there is a fundamental difference; Antony does not have the same degree of resistance to the woman, and Cleopatra is not so exclusively negative as the dark lady. In particular, *Antony and Cleopatra* is not condemned to the horrible vision of the endless circularity of lust, which is mimed in sonnet 129. Antony is subjected to some of the same oscillation betweeen "bliss" and "woe," but he is spared the flat penultimate definition of female sexuality as "this hell" (129.14). While the sonnet denies any possibility of fulfillment, Cleopatra defies such logic: "Other women cloy / The appetites they feed, but she makes hungry / Where most she satisfies" (2.2.235–37). The relentless language of calculation in the opening line of sonnet 129—"Th' expense of spirit in a waste of shame"—is transformed in *Antony and Cleopatra*. The play registers the tragic implications of Antony's "expense" and "waste" while imbuing them with the addition of a saving grace that allows *Antony and Cleopatra* to break the vicious cycle by which the poet's debasement of the woman leads automatically to his own degradation.

Antony and Cleopatra takes as its starting point the idea of woman as "strumpet" (1.1.13). Cleopatra therefore cannot be downgraded further, and the way is open for her to be "transformed" (12) upward. The image of Cleopatra as the strumpet is revived at the end of the play by Antony's momentary accusation of betrayal: "Triple-turned whore" (4.12.13). But Cleopatra turns this label aside by preventing the final drama from being staged in Rome where "I shall see / Some squeaking Cleopatra boy my greatness / I' th' posture of a whore" (5.2.219-21). This explicit reference to the boy-actor motif, bringing to our consciousness the fact that Shakespeare's Cleopatra is played by a boy, does not undercut her final claim to "greatness" as a "queen" (227), a "wife" (287), and a "lass unparallel'd" (316). Allusions to the boy-actor convention do not have the same function in all cases; the effect depends on the context. For example, the Epilogue of *As You Like It* breaks the theatrical illusion in order to expose Rosalind's female role whereas *Antony and Cleopatra* breaks the illusion in order to reaffirm it, to defend Cleopatra's status as a woman.[4] In each instance the boy-actor reference contributes to a larger development. In *As You Like It* the reference reinforces the significance of male bonding in the play as a whole; in *Antony and Cleopatra*, by ultimately protecting Cleopatra's identity as a woman and hence the heterosexual nature of Antony and Cleopatra's relationship, the reference serves to diminish the power of male bonds.

Hamlet, dying, entrusts his story and his image to the faithful Horatio, who cherishes the "sweet prince." The mortally wounded Antony entrusts his story to Cleopatra, who goes on to vindicate the trust Antony has placed in her by the eloquence of her tribute: "And there is nothing left remarkable / Beneath the visiting moon" (4.15.67–68). The counterpart of Horatio in *Antony and Cleopatra* is Enobarbus, who is unavailable in Antony's final moment but also irrelevant to it. Antony has not so much been deprived of this male bond as he has made a definitive choice in favor of the tie to Cleopatra. It is Enobarbus rather than Antony who is left to lament their separation, and Enobarbus's mourning conspicuously lacks the efficaciousness of Cleopatra's. The overall effect of Enobarbus's departure is to highlight Antony's relationship to Cleopatra and to reduce the importance of male bonds to the point where their being broken causes Antony no major regret. The Roman definition of manhood presupposes the code of male bonding that views women only as "cement" (3.2.29) to promote and consolidate male relations. Through the loss of Enobarbus and through the abiding attachment to Cleopatra, Antony enacts the rejection of this code.

II

It is easier to respond positively to Cleopatra than to Antony because he is nowhere allowed a performance as strong as Cleopatra's in the last act. Yet the two characters cannot be treated separately since the integrity of each character hinges on the integrity of their relationship as a whole. If the relationship between Cleopatra and Antony is to be convincing, it cannot be solely her creation but must in some measure be reciprocal. Cleopatra's final gesture loses its meaning if Antony is not felt to be worthy of it. Their love involves a collaboration to which Antony contributes a new male identity, the counterpart to Cleopatra's exceptional female identity. Antony's masculine identity is an essential part of the whole effect, yet it is the part that is most suspect and the reason that we are more profoundly uneasy about Antony than Cleopatra. However, we cannot begin to talk about the problem of Antony's masculinity as long as we try to fit him into tragic categories derived from earlier plays.

The effort to deal with *Antony and Cleopatra* as orthodox tragedy focuses on Antony's character and on the struggle between self-knowledge and self-delusion in relation to his choice between duty and sexual abandon, honor and love. Given this emphasis, the critic's task is to collect speeches where Antony sounds like a tragic figure and gives us glimpses of heroic self-recognition:

> But when we in our viciousness grow hard
> (O misery on't!), the wise gods seel our eyes,
> In our own filth drop our clear judgments, make us
> Adore our errors, laugh at 's while we strut
> To our confusion.
>
> (3.13.111-15)

We latch onto such passages because they seem to fit our expectations of how a tragic hero should behave, reassuring us that we know where we stand generically. Yet there are difficulties of tone and context. Antony's tragic language is slightly off-key: it is melodramatic and overstated rather than deeply anguished. The above speech too easily offers itself up for quotation, as if Antony were simply supplying that distant audience of "wise gods" with what it wanted to hear. The way in which Antony's "strut," for example, echoes Macbeth's "struts and frets" suggests disparity rather than kinship. The offhand, transient nature of Antony's utterance lacks the ultimate quality of Macbeth's genuinely desperate summation. Unable to find this concentrated pressure in *Antony and Cleopatra*, Robert Heilman questions the play's authenticity as great tragedy. But Heilman inappropriately imposes on *Antony and Cleopatra* standards he derives from earlier tragedies.[5] The classic motif of self-knowledge is a minor rather than major motif in *Antony and Cleopatra*. Rather than express disappointment by demoting the play, we should let the play generate its own standards. Then we will see that its tragic energy takes a different form.

A second disadvantage of traditional tragic concepts is that they blur the subject of gender so that it becomes impossible to analyze. The self-knowledge that Antony is alleged to evade pertains to a masculine self, whose demise is evoked through imprecise code words such as "unmanned," "effeminized," and "emasculated." This vocabulary names a taboo that discourages thought, locking criticism into an automatic consensus about the condemnation of this aspect of Antony. The notion of Antony's emasculation is a fixed point around which many interpretations turn. Antony's loss of manhood having been established, it is then possible to debate whether this sacrifice was worth it and what was gained in return. The responses range from meager to handsome acknowledgments of Antony's compensatory grandeur.

Much choric commentary can be cited to support the view that Antony's emasculation is beyond question. Antony himself, quite capable of understanding how his situation appears to an audience, can speak with this choric voice. For instance, he takes a certain relish in preempting and amplifying the Roman messenger's story:

> Speak to me home, mince not the general tongue;
> Name Cleopatra as she is call'd in Rome.
> Rail thou in Fulvia's phrase, and taunt my faults
> With such full license as both truth and malice
> Have power to utter. O then we bring forth weeds
> When our quick winds lie still, and our ills told us
> Is as our earing.
>
> $(1.2.105-11)$

These lines suggest how, in momentary self-apprehension, Antony's defiance can modulate into a self-taunting, in which "malice" is given as "full license" as "truth." Because "truth" is blended with "malice," statements of regret about Antony's loss of manhood must be evaluated rather than taken for granted. To respond to the play as a dynamic experience requires that we feel Antony's masculine identity as an open question rather than as an issue already settled in advance.

The fixed, self-evident point of Antony's emasculation needs to be reassessed. The play invites us to reconsider the traditional definition of masculinity as an identity founded on military success; the alternative is an identity responsive to qualities that the traditional image labels "feminine" and suppresses. Criticism of heroic masculinity is not unusual in Shakespeare's work: he consistently undermines the masculine self narrowly based on martial toughness. In *Othello*, for example, the rigidity, brittleness, and cost of such an identity are made painfully obvious. But Othello's need for a more inclusive definition of masculinity is implied only by its absence. What is significant about *Antony and Cleopatra* is the effort, albeit tentative and equivocal, actually to undertake a reformation of masculine identity. This view allows us to test the hypothesis that Antony's abandonment of his former heroic occupation, along with his diversion from Othello's consistency in following "the green-ey'd monster," is a positive step toward a new masculine self. It leaves open the possibility that when the pejorative Roman labels are decoded, the "emasculated" man may be one who explores his repressed "feminine" aspect.

Antony and Cleopatra draws on the art of the foregone conclusion. We are not invited to become seriously involved in the struggle between Antony's divided selves as though both sides were equal in strength because from the beginning there is a decided imbalance. Shakespeare so persistently supplies cues about Antony's inevitable return to Cleopatra and about his eventual military failure that there is little suspense about the outcome. On the contrary, the play assumes that Antony's military stature cannot be recovered. His efforts are so patently grandiose, empty gestures that we hardly need Enobarbus to make this point. Antony remains torn betweeen old and new versions of masculinity, vacillating to the very end. From the traditional point of view there are periodic expressions of helplessness such as "She has robb'd me of my sword" (4.14.23). There is the ultimate attempt to maintain a veneer of the old heroic image when he interprets his suicide as proof that his orthodox honor is intact: "and do now not basely die, / Not cowardly put off my helmet to / My countryman—a Roman by a Roman / Valiantly vanquish'd" (4.15.55–58). But the main action of the play is gradually but relentlessly to strip away this former reputation and to bring Antony to "the very heart of loss" (4.12.29). Paradoxically, Antony's essential destiny is not to recover his military identity but to lose it. It is important to formulate the dramatic action in this way because it frees us from an inappropriate concentration on the moral that Antony should not have made the mistake of committing himself to Cleopatra and permits us instead to see that the "mistake" is crucial in enabling the experiment in alternative masculinity to proceed. There is something positive in Antony's impulse to give himself away because much of the search for a new masculine identity involves shedding the old identity. The play's genuine suspense can be relocated in the troubling questions about the validity and final status of this experiment.

Antony's relationship to Cleopatra can be read in two ways simultaneously. The negative version sees gender-role reversal: Cleopatra plays controlling woman to Antony's vitiated masculinity. In the positive version, Antony and Cleopatra engage in a gender-role exchange that enlarges but does not erase the original and primary sexual identity of each. Both versions are necessary to the complete dramatic experience since this double reading of gender helps to produce the painful ambivalence that characterizes our response to the play. However, I shall concentrate here on the latter version because its complexity deserves elaboration. Antony and Cleopatra do not satisfactorily attain the ideal of extending one's given sexual identity by incorporating the identity of the opposite sex; but their attempt must be felt as a noble aspiration, and not mere delusion, if the play is to have its full impact.

Gender-role exchange in *Antony and Cleopatra* does not cancel Antony's basic identity as a man or Cleopatra's as a woman, nor does it dissolve the boundary between "male" and "female." Instead, what is involved is crossing back and forth over a boundary no longer seen as a rigid barrier dividing the two sexes into two absolutely separate groups.[6] This capacity for cross-gender identification—*heterosexual androgyny*—distinguishes it from the androgyny in the service of male bonds in *As You Like It* and from the relative heterosexual polarization in *The Winter's Tale*. The concept of *heterosexual androgyny* defines the context in which Cleopatra can, without contradiction and without ceasing to be female, refer to herself as both a man and a woman: "No more but e'en a woman" (4.15.73) and "I have nothing / Of woman in me" (5.2.238–39). But in Antony's case such range of gender reference is more problematic. Shakespeare's use of transvestism exemplifies the problem: women who put on male dress are as a general rule enhanced whereas men in women's clothes, such as Falstaff disguised as the old woman of Brainford in *The Merry Wives of Windsor*, feel humiliated. When Cleopatra, trying to reassure herself in Antony's absence, recalls how she "put my tires and mantles on him, whilst / I wore his sword Philippan" (2.5.22–23), her image seems only to arouse and confirm the fears already expressed by Octavius that Antony "is not more manlike / Than Cleopatra; nor the queen of Ptolomy / More womanly than he" (1.4.5–7). However, these entirely pejorative connotations of Antony's taking on a womanly identity are not the whole story, for the play also gives his role playing as a woman a more absorbing and plausible dramatization than the simple negative view allows. In particular, Antony's identification with maternal bounty gives his masculinity its liberatory, subversive quality.

III

The combination of tragic cost and redeeming psychological value in *Antony and Cleopatra* is dramatized in the motif of bounty. This motif and the related imagery of eating have been well discussed by such critics as Eugene Waith and Maurice Charney.[7] Their analyses can be extended by viewing the concept of bounty in the larger framework of maternal nurturance. Sonnet 143, for example, suggests that a key to the dark woman's identity can be found in the poet's self-image as "her neglected child" (143.5), who is caught between the desire for maternal "kindness" (143.12) and the disappointment of maternal abandonment. The exposition of the vehicle and tenor of the metaphor unfolds so simply, the poet's stance is so plangently vulnerable, the scene seems so farfetched that it is hard to know how to interpret this sonnet. The usual hostility and bitterness are absent, and for once the poet addresses the woman with the special pleading reserved for the youth. The feeling of total dependence expressed in relation to the young man is, in this moment, redirected, explicitly indicating the motherly response he desires from the lady.

Cleopatra is another woman who, to use the language of sonnet 143, "plays the mother's part."[8] The maternal orientation of her role is conveyed by the imagery of food, which is often used to describe her sexual relationship with Antony; the oral mode of this relationship links it with maternal feeding. The otherwise puzzling assertion that "she makes hungry / Where most she satisfies" (2.2.236–37) can be understood by shifting from sexual to maternal contexts and imagining nurturant symbiosis as a model for physical bliss. As Lear's prison speech envisions a world unto itself in which he and Cordelia are isolated together, so Antony seeks a place where the political vicissitudes of "Who loses and who wins; who's in, who's out" (*Lear*, 5.3.15) are irrelevant: "Here is my space" (*Antony*, 1.1.34). But Lear and Antony reclaim maternal bounty in strikingly different ways. Lear responds to the maternal possibilities outside himself embodied in Cordelia's capacity to provide the enveloping security of "kind nursery." Antony does not rely exclusively on Cleopatra for his image of the maternal but instead finds the maternal within himself. His energies are not devoted solely to casting the woman in a maternal role: he himself actively and recklessly "plays the mother's part." His lavish prodigality, though indiscriminate and capricious, suggests an attempt to imitate maternal bounty, to become the ideal, all-giving mother. No claim is made here that Antony consciously formulates this project; rather, such a project is implicit in the imagery and dramatic structure by which his apparently random behavior is organized and given direction.

The customary critical portrait of Antony that keeps separate the negative aspect of effeminization and the compensatory positive aspect of magnanimity cannot be sustained. Antony's celebrated generosity is not unrelated to his fluidity with regard to gender. What we call his magnanimity is, in effect, an effort to reorder his psychic economy and to reallocate gender roles so that he gains direct rather than vicarious access to unrestricted maternal giving. Though Antony is destroyed by his adoption of maternal behavior, his effort is not entirely negative because it ultimately leads to the establishment of a convincing reciprocal relationship with Cleopatra, of an extraordinary depth of collaboration. Here again, the parallel between *King Lear* and *Antony and Cleopatra* does not hold because Lear destroys the potential for mutuality with Cordelia when he constructs his dream vision of their life in prison: Cordelia does not participate in the creation of this vision.

Cleopatra's first meeting with Antony is conducted in terms of food:

> Upon her landing, Antony sent to her,
> Invited her to supper. She replied,
> It should be better he became her guest;
> Which she entreated. Our courteous Antony,
> Whom ne'er the word of "No" woman heard speak,
> Being barber'd ten times o'er, goes to the feast;
> And for his ordinary pays his heart
> For what his eyes eat only.
>
> (2.2.219–26)

By countering Antony's invitation with the proposal that she play the role of provider, Cleopatra gains control of the situation as the verb "pays" (225) makes plain. Antony's preference for the image of extravagance that Cleopatra presents is clear from the outset. His gift of the "orient pearl," symbolizing the promise that " 'I will piece / Her opulent throne with kingdoms' " (1.5.41,45–46), suggests his attempt to repay Cleopatra with a grandness that equals hers. In Rome, Antony's bounty is constrained by his reconciliation with Octavius. As soon as he receives Caesar's gift of his sister, Antony realizes that his liberality with respect to Pompey must be curtailed (2.2.153—55), as his subsequent address to Pompey confirms: "I have heard it, Pompey / And am well studied for a liberal thanks, / Which I do owe you" (2.6.46–48). The verb "studied" suggests the fraudulence of Antony's "liberal thanks" and shows how unattractive Caesar's kind of withholding can make Antony look. His final break with Caesar occurs when the latter invalidates Antony's reputation by refusing to give it the requisite verbal testimony:

> Spoke scantly of me; when perforce he could not
> But pay me terms of honor, cold and sickly
> He vented them, most narrow measure lent me;
> When the best hint was given him, he not took't,
> Or did it from his teeth.
>
> $\qquad$ (3.4.6–10)

Antony's complaint about Caesar's inadequate payment is literally elaborated in a set of formal "accusations" (3.6.23), which make clear how much honor is a matter of businesslike distribution of spoils (24–37). Antony retaliates by confounding this logic of computation with an unrestrained display of liberality toward Cleopatra:

> I' th' market-place, on a tribunal silver'd,
> Cleopatra and himself in chairs of gold
> Were publicly enthron'd. . . .
>
> $\qquad$ Unto her
> He gave the stablishment of Egypt, made her
> Of lower Syria, Cyprus, Lydia,
> Absolute queen.
>
> $\qquad$ (3–6, 8–11)

Plutarch's *Life of Marcus Antonius* opens with an anecdote about Antony's father, who was

specially very liberal in giving, as appeareth by an act he did. He was not very wealthy, and therefore his wife would not let him use his liberality and frank nature. One day a friend of his coming to him to pray him to help him to some money, having great need, Antonius by chance had no money to give him, but he commanded one of his men to bring him some water in a silver basin, and after he had brought it him he washed his beard as though he meant to have shaven it, and then found an errand for his man to send him out, and gave his friend the silver basin, and bade him get him money with that. Shortly after there was a great stir among the servants, seeking out this silver basin; insomuch as Antonius seeing his wife marvellously offended for it, and that she would examine all her servants one after another about it, to know what was become of it, at length he confessed he had given it away, and prayed her to be contented.[9]

The story hints that the father's liberality is double-edged; although this generosity is impressively large-spirited, it is also potentially imprudent to the point of self-destruction. Plutarch then shows how this potential is made actual in the case of Antony. His liberality inextricably links genuine magnanimity and willful prodigality. Unlike the father's wife, Cleopatra stimulates rather than restrains the impulse to squander himself. Antony's act of giving kingdoms to Cleopatra (3.6) is soon followed by his giving away in advance the victory at Actium to Caesar. The whimsical decision to fight at sea ensures Antony's defeat because, as Enobarbus points out: "you therein throw away / The absolute soldiership you have by land" (3.7.41–42). The idea of liberality modulates into the more explicitly reckless notion of "throwing away." Antony's generosity is indiscriminate and out of control: it is as though, with his casual freewheeling manner, he is setting himself up to lose. His reaction after the first defeat is interesting for the readiness and finality with which he embraces it. He says all the right things about deeply regretting his shame. But, at the same time, the insistence with which he encourages his friends to abandon him suggests that he is anxious to get on with the real business of loss. He is so generous that he will reward his men for leaving him and hastening his demise:

> I have a ship
> Laden with gold, take that, divide it; fly,
> And make your peace with Caesar.
> . . . Friends, be gone,
> I have myself resolv'd on a course
> Which has no need of you. Be gone.
> My treasure's in the harbor; take it. . . .
> Friends, be gone. . . .
> I will possess you of that ship and treasure.
> (3.11.4–6, 8–11, 15, 21)

Antony's deepest impulse is to give up, and his liberality is a conveniently noble means to that end.

The first two scenes of act 4 present contrasting pictures of Caesar and Antony before the second battle. What Caesar views in his pinched way as "waste" (4.1.16), Antony sees expansively as bounty: "let's tonight / Be bounteous at our meal" (4.2.9–10). Antony's ostensible purpose is to celebrate the recovery of his confidence, but his extravagant desire for "one other gaudy night" (3.13.182) exudes desperation. When he summons his servants to prepare for the feast, he slides into a farewell speech:

> Tend me to-night;
> May be it is the period of your duty;
> Haply you shall not see me more, or if,
> A mangled shadow. Perchance to-morrow
> You'll serve another master. I look on you
> As one that takes his leave.
>
> (4.2.24–29)

After Enobarbus chides him, Antony tries to retract the fatalism of his address and to sound buoyantly optimistic: "Ho, ho, ho! / Now the witch take me, if I meant it thus!" (36–37). But the impact of his self-image as "A mangled shadow" remains. The effect is not to evoke renewed hope, but momentarily to conceal its absence by "drowning consideration" (45). The feast promotes the dissipation of identity to which Antony instinctively gravitates. His brief flash of triumph—capped by the lavish dispensing of gold armor to the wounded Scarus (4.8.22–29)—does not alter the growing impression that Antony's defeat is inevitable. His temporary success is preceded by parallel losses in act 4, scenes 3 and 5: the departures of Hercules and Enobarbus. The undeniably generous response to Enobarbus's defection needs to be placed in the whole sequence of Antony's demonstrative gestures; the sending of Enobarbus's treasure after him with "bounty overplus" (4.6.21) is another step in Antony's divesting himself of power.

This process of stripping away is explicitly incorporated into Antony's self-image at the moment when his destiny is final. After issuing to Scarus the order for the dispersal, which has in fact already occurred—"Bid them all fly; / . . . Bid them all fly, be gone" (4.12.15, 17)—Antony, in soliloquy, claims for himself the image of a tree stripped of its bark: "and this pine is bark'd / That overtopp'd them all" (23–24). With this image articulated, he can go on consciously to fulfill it by stripping himself of his armor. Having attained "the very heart of loss," Antony begins to experience the complete dissolution of identity imaged in the cloud (4.14.2–11), though at the same time the cloud's rapid shape-shifting creates "black vesper's pageants" (8) and suggests the principle of transformation. Antony's prodigal and dissolute behavior has conspired to bring about this outcome, which he now actively pursues. "This visible shape" (14), which he feels he "cannot hold," becomes the armor that he now dismantles: "Unarm, Eros . . . / No more a soldier. Bruised pieces, go" (35,42). In renouncing his soldier identity, Antony also rejects the definition of masculinity that it entails. In psychological terms, the armor symbolizes emotional defenses, which Antony willingly gives up. His allusion to Dido and "her Aeneas" (53) indicates the positive self-definition initiated by disarming; Antony refuses the epic masculinity that requires the abandonment of love in favor of empire.

However, after his death, the story of Antony is in Cleopatra's hands. She has the power to make his self-image as a heroic lover a mockery or a truth that must be honored. Antony's claim to be "her Aeneas" is meaningless unless Cleopatra agrees to become his Dido. Whether she will take such reciprocal action remains in doubt until the very end. In the beginning, by taunting him with the idea of calculation, Cleopatra elicits from Antony a statement of unbounded love:

CLEO. If it be love indeed, tell me how much.
ANT. There's beggary in the love that can be reckon'd.
CLEO. I'll set a bourn how far to be belov'd.
ANT. Then must thou needs find out new heaven, new earth.

(1.1.14–17)

Because Antony's decisive commitment is not matched by similar language from Cleopatra, their relationship is an uncertain one. In the moment when it seems that she is about to give an equivalent testimony, she lacks language:

Sir, you and I must part, but that's not it;
Sir, you and I have lov'd, but there's not it;
That you know well. Something it is I would—
O, my oblivion is a very Antony,
And I am all forgotten.

(1.3.87–91)

But through mourning, she discovers the words to bear witness to the "Something it is I would." Having nothing left to give, Antony gives to Cleopatra the gift of his dying self. He has disintegrated into Osiris-like fragments, and in grieving for him, Cleopatra reconstructs his image on a colossal scale. In particular, she endows him with the quality of "bounty":

For his bounty
There was no winter in't; an autumn it was
That grew the more by reaping. His delights
Were dolphin-like, they show'd his back above
The element they liv'd in. In his livery

Walk'd crowns and crownets; realms and islands were
As plates dropped from his pocket.

(5.2.86–92)

The dramatic force of this passage is increased by the motif of competing fictions. Against Cleopatra's dream of Antony's bounty stands the bounty offered to her by Octavius. Proculeius announces that Caesar's "bounty" (5.2.43) "o'erflows the measure" (1.1.2): "Make your full reference freely to my lord, / Who is so full of grace that it flows over / On all that need" (5.2.23–25). Caesar's real motive—"for her life in Rome / Would be eternal in our triumph" (5.1.65–66)—of course makes his promise of bounty mere pretense.

Cleopatra's image of Antony's unending profusion replaces Octavius's preferred version of his heroic deprivation:

When thou once
Was beaten from Modena, where thou slew'st
Hirtius and Pansa, consuls, at thy heel
Did famine follow, whom thou fought'st against
(Though daintily brought up) with patience more
Than savages could suffer. Thou didst drink
The stale of horses and the gilded puddle
Which beasts would cough at; thy palate then did
  deign
The roughest berry on the rudest hedge;
Yea, like the stag, when snow the pasture sheets,
The barks of trees thou brows'd. On the Alps
It is reported thou didst eat strange flesh
Which some did die to look on.

(1.4.56–68)

While Octavius finds in Antony a heightened image of his own abstemiousness, Cleopatra's celebration of the bountiful Antony projects a model in which she discovers her own bounty. Cleopatra's gesture of giving Antony's "chronicle" enacts her answer to his generosity.[10] Her tribute simultaneously conveys the tragic consequences of his liberality and her redemption of it. Cleopatra will shortly give her own life in order to validate this "dream" (5.2.74, 76). The mutuality that Antony had evoked at the, outset—"such a mutual pair" (1.1.37)—is belatedly confirmed by Caesar's recognition of "A pair so famous" (5.2.360). The thoroughness of their mutuality, especially Antony's part in it, is underestimated if all the credit is given to Cleopatra. His maternal action is as indispensable as hers to the overall effect.

IV

When using *Antony and Cleopatra* as a signpost that marks a turning point in Shakespeare's artistic career, it is convenient to call it a "transitional play," halfway between tragedy and late romance. But this very convenience is a danger because a fifty-fifty formulation makes it easy to tip the balance toward the future development of the romance at the expense of the tragic element. Robert Ornstein's "The Ethic of the Imagination: Love and Art in 'Antony and Cleopatra' " is a sophisticated, eloquent, and moving celebration of the artistic alliance of Shakespeare with Cleopatra at the end of the play: "It is the artist in Cleopatra who stirs Shakespeare's deepest imaginative sympathies and who receives the immeasurable bounty of his artistic love, which is immortality itself."[11] In this summation, the tragic note is downplayed to the point of being lost; the fact of death is nullified through transcendence: "the metamorphosis of her death, which turns life into art."[12]

Faced with critical hyperbole so thoroughly identified with the lovers' point of view that it reproduces Cleopatra's hyperbole, one looks for help in the grudging antiromantic criticism of Robert Heilman, whose acerbic conclusion contains a grain of truth: Cleopatra's finale represents "the ultimate creation of the male erotic dream . . . the soul of the promiscuous woman faithful, in the end, to oneself alone."[13] What Heilman usefully reminds us is that the play's "dream" cuts both ways: it signifies, as Ornstein argues, the power of artistic salvation, but it also signifies, as Heilman insists, the wishful thinking debunked by the soothsayer: "If every of your wishes had a womb, / And fertile every wish, a million" (1.2.38–39). The final dramatization of Antony and Cleopatra's relationship intertwines the elements of escapist fantasy and authentic transfiguration. Yet sympathetic critics refuse to allow their hopes to be disappointed, and disaffected critics, holding themselves safely aloof from the dramatic experience, refuse to feel hope in the first place. But the play's effect includes both the engagement of our hope and its disappointment, moving in a dialectical process that begins with experiment and ends in failure.[14] The experiment envisages a reformulation of masculine identity in the context of a sustainable androgynous heterosexuality, an experiment we desperately want to succeed in this play. Our need to believe is so strong that the romantic version is hard to resist. However, the full experience of the play is the complete sequence, ending in the recognition that Antony and Cleopatra are not entirely successful in fashioning a new, wholly positive mode of relationship between men and women. This hurts. But just as we cannot avoid taking the risk of letting our hope to be aroused, so we cannot avoid the hurt.

The formal structure of *Antony and Cleopatra* inverts the normal comic pattern. To use C. L. Barber's terms, the play moves from "release" to resistance. It begins in festive Egypt ("There's not a minute of our lives should stretch / Without some pleasure now" [1.1.46–47]), shifts to Rome, and ends in Egypt because Cleopatra frustrates Octavius's goal of bringing her to Rome. The middle space normally occupied by the liberating pastoral environment is given to the stringent "real world" of Rome. Because the final phase is a return to Egypt rather than to this real world, the usual "clarification" about love—"putting holiday in perspective with life as a whole"[15]—is placed under an extreme and complex dramatic pressure. Ordinarily, the conclusion holds out the prospect of rejoining the festive and reality principles so that characters return to an everyday society now rejuvenated by the pastoral excursion. But in *Antony and Cleopatra* the two worlds remain sharply split. Consequently, we are left at the end with a painfully divided response, for which there is no resolution.

The lyricism of the ending is sometimes used to mitigate the full brunt of the tragedy; but this approach depends on a false opposition of poetry and rigor, for the poetry itself is rigorous. In the final scene Cleopatra affirms her "greatness" by elevating herself from the category of strumpet to the status of "queen" and "lass unparallel'd" (5.2.227, 316). Yet Shakespeare does not go to the other extreme of proposing her unqualified idealization. Cleopatra is not permitted in the end to "make defect perfection" (2.2.231). Her aspiration—"I am fire and air; my other elements / I give to baser life" (5.2.289–90)—is placed by the earthbound imagery of the final commentary. She imagines "a better life" in which she "never palates more the dung, / The beggar's nurse and Caesar's" (2,7–8); yet in seeking "heaven" (303), her poetic sensibility finds its way unerringly back to the nurse image. Death is not an incidental tragic overlay but endemic to the love relationship in a way the specific form of her death reveals: "Dost thou not see the baby at my breast, / That sucks the nurse asleep?" (309–10). Cleopatra's apotheosis explicitly converts the maternal image from life-giving nurturance into an "easy way to die" (356), poignant but nonetheless destructive. The logic of transformation in *Antony and Cleopatra* is finally incomplete and imperfect because a totally benign image of maternal feeding, purged of all association with anxiety-producing doubt, cannot be achieved. Shakespeare goes a long way toward a major reformulation of masculine identity by having Antony participate actively in maternal bounty instead of merely being its filial beneficiary or its paternal manager. However, Shakespeare precludes a harmonious conclusion to Antony's direct contact,

through identification, with the maternal. The final manifestation of maternal beneficence, uncomfortably undercut
by Cleopatra's equation of baby with poisonous asp, exposes Antony's lavish giving as the enactment of men's
fantasy of motherhood, a fantasy whose idealized fulfillment the play disallows.

One way around the unhappy impediments in Antony and Cleopatra's relationship is to stress their positive qualities relative to Octavius, whose glaring defects
provide an easy target for criticism, the better to elevate
Antony and Cleopatra to a position of comparative superiority. But I do not think that we can draw as much
consolation from this comparative perspective as do
those romantic critics who use it as evidence that Shakespeare endorses the lovers. It is unsatisfactory to rest the
case on this comparison if it diverts our attention from
problems within the lovers' relationship, considered in
and of itself.

Furthermore, Shakespeare's use of Octavius is not entirely favorable to Antony and Cleopatra. Though Shakespeare generously sponsors the final reconciliation of Antony and Cleopatra, Octavius stands as an absolute limit to
this generosity. Nor should we see Octavius's role at the
end as simply calculated realism by which Shakespeare
checks an excessive endorsement of the lovers. However
"paltry," Octavius's presence is formidable and can be
taken to signify Shakespeare's self-division. The festive
conclusion Octavius imagines himself instituting—"The
time of universal peace is near" (4.6.4)—is compromised
not only because this harmony remains outside the bounds
of the play, but also because the cynical attitude Octavius
displays toward women—"Women are not / In their best
fortunes strong, but want will perjure / The ne'er-touched
vestal" (3.12.29–31)—would be incorporated into the
structure of his "universal" peace. Nonetheless, Octavius's undeniable political success allows Shakespeare to
hedge his bets, to limit the gamble he makes on Cleopatra.

Whatever "the odds" (2.3.28, 39; 4.15.66), Shakespeare takes no chances and carefully circumscribes the risk in his commitment to the lovers' project: unlike Antony and Cleopatra, he makes no unconditional gesture. Rather, through the person of Octavius, Shakespeare keeps his distance and his ambivalence. Protected by the irrefutable reality principle Octavius represents, Shakespeare can legitimately insist on the escapist aspect of Antony and Cleopatra's suicidal action and thus regard them with a safe mixture of admiration and criticism.

The Limitations of Reformed Masculinity in *The Winter's Tale*

A critical assessment of *The Winter's Tale* can benefit greatly from a focus on the ways sexual politics shapes the interaction of the characters. *Sexual politics* refers to the characters' assumptions about what it means to be masculine or feminine and to the relative power that accrues to these implicit definitions of gender. Patriarchy forms one basis for the relations within the play, and the need to maintain and renew it amounts to a central motif. The dramatic action consists partly in the fashioning of a benign patriarchy—in the transition from a brutal, crude, tyrannical version to a benevolent one capable of including and valuing women.[1] *The Winter's Tale* enacts the disruption and revival of patriarchy: the male-oriented social order undergoes a series of challenges and crises that reveal how unstable it is until it can be reestablished on a new basis.

The most obvious disturbance in male control is the abrupt manifestation of Leontes's alienation from Hermione. Othello's "soul and body" are "ensnar'd" by a "demi-devil" (5.2.301–2), but Leontes's spontaneous outburst of jealousy does not require prompting from an external villain but is instead intrinsic to the male psyche. The place of Iago is here filled by Hermione's pregnancy, which is very visible and in and of itself acts as a provocation to male insecurity: "Spread of late / Into a goodly bulk" (2.1.19–20). Hermione activates a maternal image in the most literal way possible. This difference between

Hermione and Desdemona is crucial. Leontes is not threatened by woman per se as Othello is; the threat takes the more specific and acute form of woman as mother.

Leontes's apposition and thus connection of "bounty" with "fertile bosom" suggest the maternal role in which he casts his wife:

> This entertainment
> May a free face put on, derive a liberty
> From heartiness, from bounty, fertile bosom,
> And well become the agent; 't may—I grant.
> (1.2.111–14)

The "bounty" provided by maternal "entertainment" is suddenly suspect and inherently untrustworthy. Once the "free face" of nurturance appears to be a mask falsely "put on," Leontes's belief collapses, and his own facial composure disintegrates. Polixenes reports that Leontes "hath on him such a countenance / As he had lost some province and a region / Lov'd as he loves himself" (368–70). Leontes cannot even follow Camillo's advice to pretend that all is well: "Go then; and with a countenance as clear / As friendship wears at feasts, keep with Bohemia / And with your queen" (343-45). Leontes's aggressive doubt renders "friendship" and "feasts" impossible, and the image of festivity does not reappear until the pastoral scene in act 4 from which Leontes is absent.

I

Even before a woman enters, the play dramatizes a problem in male institutions. The opening phase (from 1.1.1 to 1.2.27, when Leontes turns in frustration to Hermione) shows that the politics of male "entertainment" (1.1.8) is strained. The verbal exchange between Camillo and Archidamus (1.1), which anticipates the similar exchange (at the beginning of 1.2) between the two men they represent, reveals an uneasiness beneath the elaborate surface politeness. The tension stems from the disparity in the two kings' munificence; mutuality is threatened because the two cannot give equally. Archidamus insists, despite Camillo's efforts to dissuade him, that Bohemia cannot match Sicilia's "magnificence" (1.1.12) and that therefore "our entertainment shall shame us" (8).[2] So burdened is the idea of Polixenes's having to reciprocate Leontes's hospitality that Leontes's anticipated visit to Bohemia never takes place. Camillo tries to remove entertainment from the realm of calculation and to view it as pure generosity and love: "You pay a great deal too dear for what's given freely" (17–18). Yet he does not succeed, as the direct exchange between Leontes and Polixenes shows.

In retrospect, we note a sharp contrast between past and present circumstances. In Polixenes's paradisal version of his childhood friendship with Leontes, the two had traded "innocence for innocence" (1.2.69). This mode of exchange has now been replaced by an "interchange of gifts, letters, loving embassies" (1.1.28), which is expanded to include "entertainment" (8), a general display of largesse, when Polixenes's visit temporarily ends "separation of their society" (26). The defects in this form of exchange emerge at the sensitive point when the visit draws to a close. The intricacies of protocol express contentiousness as much as affection. Polixenes, echoing Archidamus, announces his inability to repay:

> Time as long again
> Would be fill'd up, my brother, with our thanks,
> And yet we should, for perpetuity,
> Go hence in debt.
>
> (1.2.3–6)

Both giving and accepting become obligatory as Leontes's insistence on his liberality grows into an imposition. The barely suppressed tension in the situation comes out in odd language: "We are tougher, brother, / Than you can put us to 't" (15–16); and "which to hinder / Were (in your love) a whip to me; my stay, / To you a charge and trouble" (24–26). Leontes gets his way, but he also gets this "trouble." In Marcel Mauss's formulation, "charity wounds" the recipient;[3] but Leontes's charity wounds Leontes himself.

The initial discord is a product of male interaction rather than of female intrusion. When Leontes draws his wife into this competitive situation, she expresses the preexisting mood in a playful and heightened way, speaking vividly and openly about the emotional ambivalence of the guest–host relation. Her imagery picks up and magnifies Polixenes's reference to the "whip," as she stresses the aggressive, combative side of munificence: "He's beat from his best ward" (1.2.33), and "We'll thwack him hence with distaffs" (37). Her wit is quite blunt about the coerciveness of courtesy: "Force me to keep you as a prisoner, / Not like a guest: so you shall pay your fees / When you depart, and save your thanks" (52-54).

After Hermione has "won" (1.2.86) Polixenes's consent to extend his visit, Leontes effusively congratulates her. But, his competitive instinct aroused, he immediately contrasts his wife's success with his own failure: "At my request he would not" (87). However, Hermione's victory is more apparent than real. Polixenes's deference to her comes from his unwillingness to "offend" (57) a woman, a form of politeness that constricts as much as it enhances her power. Hermione succeeds in breaking the stalemate between the two men because Polixenes is receptive to any woman who can call forth his courtly reflex gesture (56–59). "O my most sacred lady" (77) is the automatic response to a woman who is regarded as the source from whom it is blessed to receive. Although Polixenes's response to women is inconsistent, as Hermione quickly points out (80–82), there is a familiar method in his inconsistency. While Renaissance men aspire to the ideal of the whole man, women are typically divided into opposite extremes: perfection and evil. Thus, Polixenes calls Hermione "sacred" at the same time that he implies that women are "devils" (82) who spoil idealized male bonds (67–79).

The constriction in Hermione's power emerges when she moves from repartee with Polixenes to direct contention with Leontes. Having proven that "a lady's 'verily' is / As potent as a lord's" (1.2.50-51) and having exposed the pretention of Polixenes's nostalgic "boy eternal" (65), she issues a sharp challenge to her husband:

> What? have I twice said well? When was't before?
> I prithee tell me; cram's with praise and make's
> As fat as tame things. One good deed dying
>   tongueless
> Slaughters a thousand waiting upon that.
> Our praises are our wages.
>
> (90–94)

The sarcastic tone turns her performance sour, calling attention to the limits of her wit. She provokes Leontes into naming the moment when she yielded to his courtship and became his possession by "clapping thyself my love" and "uttering, / 'I am yours forever' " (104–5). Her dependent status as a receiver of male praise originates in this gesture of submission. She can mock her identity as a "tame thing" (92), but she can neither transgress nor change it. Hermione's entrapment in her marital role thus precedes and prefigures her literal imprisonment by the " 'jealous tyrant' " (3.2.133–34). After losing Leontes's "favor"—"the crown and comfort of my life" (94)—she appeals to a divine authority, which is male: "Apollo be my judge!" (116).[4] And she submits her case to an earlier patriarchal authority:

> The Emperor of Russia was my father.
> O that he were alive, and here beholding
> His daughter's trial! that he did but see
> The flatness of my misery, yet with eyes
> Of pity, not revenge!
>
> (119–123)

This recourse to the benign father provides a microcosm of the play's resolution. It points ahead to Leontes's conversion from vengefulness to benevolence and establishes the female commitment, not to independence, but to patriarchal power properly used.

Hermione's triumph in persuading Polixenes to remain in Sicilia is short-lived. By the end of act 1, scene 2, Polixenes reverses his promise to her and immediately departs with Camillo by the "posterns" (438, 464). Hermione is defenseless not only because of Leontes's "tyranny" (3.2.31) but because of the other men's speedy exit. Although Polixenes utters pieties about Hermione's innocence—"comfort / The gracious queen, part of his theme, but nothing / Of his ill-ta'en suspicion!" (1.2.458–60)—the effect of his watchword—"Let us avoid" (462)—is to abandon Hermione to her own devices. This abandonment by men accentuates the sexual division of labor, forcing us to notice that her devices are specifically feminine ones.

In the final scene of the play Hermione becomes the "most sacred lady" who restores the image of "bounty" (1.2.113) that Leontes so drastically questions. The play achieves this restoration by distinguishing male and female kinds of gift-giving. Male gift-giving is institutionalized, though it has its "natural" source in Polixenes's image of "twinn'd lambs that did frisk i' th' sun" (67). But this portrait of ideal male bonds owes less to nature than to the conventions of pastoral artifice. As an expression of male imagination, Polixenes's fantasy is linked to subsequent instances of false male dreams in the play. In particular, Leontes's "dreams" (3.2.82) enact a parody of procreation: "With what's unreal thou co-active art, / And fellow'st nothing" (1.2.141–42). Female bounty, in contrast, is analogous to nature, grounded in giving birth and nurturance to infants. The three women in the play appear to function not according to the logic Marcel Mauss outlines but rather with the liberality that Edgar Wind attributes to the three graces.[5]

These two structures of giving are illustrated by the two kinds of innocence in which they originate. Polixenes as-

serts the pastoral innocence of his and Leontes's friendship—insulated from women: "What we chang'd / Was
innocence for innocence" (1.2.68–69). Once this friendship
is poisoned by Leontes's suspicion, another form of innocence emerges in connection with the birth of Perdita. Paulina sees the baby as "pure innocence" (2.2.39). Hermione
defends herself by association with her daughter—"My
poor prisoner, / I am innocent as you" (26–27)—and protests that her baby "is from my breast / (The innocent milk
in it most innocent mouth) / Hal'd out to murther"
(3.2.99–101). Here is the "fertile bosom" that Leontes's
delusory mistrust negates. Finally, the oracle confirms that
the child is an "innocent babe" (135). The plot formula
contained in the phrase "if that which is lost be not found"
(135) suggests that the recovery of Perdita means recovery
of the values associated with her: the mutually reinforcing
innocence of the newborn and of the maternal bounty
symbolized by literal nurturance ("innocent milk"). To
summarize, the plot involves the hopeless corruption of
the giving instituted in male entertainment, the reconstitu-
tion of the concept of entertainment through festive occasions that center on women (on Perdita in 4.4, on Paulina
and Hermione in 5.3) and serve as analogues of maternal
nurturance, and the eventual return of entertainment to
male control.

Having lost Hermione and Polixenes and unable
to prevail upon Camillo to serve as an accomplice, Leontes is left with an emotional vacuum he tries to fill by
turning to Mamillius. Mamillius becomes his new
"twinn'd lamb" (1.2.67), as Leontes invokes the father–
son identification that reinforces patriarchal succession
and uses it to escape from the intolerable and genital
present:

> Looking on the lines
> Of my boy's face, methoughts I did recoil
> Twenty-three years, and saw myself unbreech'd
> In my green velvet coat, my dagger muzzled,

Lest it should bite its master, and so prove
(As ornament oft does) too dangerous.
(153–58)

In thus sanctioning his "recoil," Leontes reverses the equation that promotes continuity: instead of the son's becoming the father, the father becomes the son, swallowing up Mamillius in the process.

Leontes's use of his son as a narcissistic reflector on whom to project his own anxieties becomes the pattern for his actions. After concluding that "I have drunk, and seen the spider" (2.1.45), Leontes immediately moves to protect Mamillius from oral contamination by separating mother and son: "Give me the boy. I am glad you did not nurse him" (56). Leontes's use of Mamillius as an unacknowledged mirror image is again evident in his diagnosis of his son's disease:

> To see his nobleness,
> Conceiving the dishonor of his mother!
> He straight declin'd, droop'd, took it deeply,
> Fasten'd and fix'd the shame on't in himself,
> Threw off his spirit, his appetite, his sleep,
> And downright languish'd.
> (2.3.12–17)

This description fits the revulsion Leontes feels on "conceiving" Hermione's "dishonor." He opens the scene complaining of symptoms similar to those of his son, including insomnia: "Nor night, nor day, no rest" (1). He fails completely in his attempt to nurture his son. Preoccupied with himself, he cannot see that his son's depression stems from maternal deprivation, which causes the boy's death.

Confronted by Paulina, Leontes attacks her husband. Like Mamillius, Antigonus is a screen on whom Leontes projects his anxieties. We hear Leontes's accusations against Antigonus as self-accusations and self-doubts: "What? canst not rule her?" (2.3.46); "Thou dotard, thou art woman-tir'd; unroosted / By thy Dame Partlet here"

(75–76); and "He dreads his wife" (80). Leontes's decision not to burn the newborn baby, his willingness to "let it live" (157), coincides with his decision to punish Antigonus: "You that have been so tenderly officious / With Lady Margery, your midwife there, / . . . what will you adventure / To save this brat's life?" (159–60, 162–63). In the long run, Leontes himself learns to be "tenderly officious." In the short run, he assigns "adventure" to Antigonus. Leontes thus delegates his problems to Antigonus, who, like a scapegoat, takes on the suffering that Leontes would have had to endure if the play were a tragedy. "O, the sacrifice," marvel the visitors to Apollo's temple (3.1.6). In the play as a whole, Mamillius and Antigonus are sacrificed to exorcise Leontes's wrath, to propitiate the terrible mother created by Leontes's fears.

Paulina conforms to this fear, in effect, by impersonating the mother figure that haunts Leontes. In adopting Perdita's cause, Paulina becomes a foster mother, a surrogate for the imprisoned Hermione. The maternal link between Hermione and Paulina, emphasized by Paulina's carrying the baby on stage, helps to explain Leontes's extreme reaction. Paulina continues the mother–child image from which Leontes is estranged: he sees Paulina's nurturance ("I / Do come with words as medicinal as true" [2.3.36–37]) as a poison he must resist at all costs.

From the standpoint of sexual politics, the relation between mother and son is a special one not easily integrated into the patriarchal order. The reversal of sexual roles to which Leontes strenuously objects in the Paulina–Antigonus relation is normal in the mother–infant bond. In theory, the husband's power over the wife contains and restrains the mother's power over the male child. But this set of checks and balances breaks down if the husband's anxiety leads him to adopt sonlike postures (as I argue Leontes does). In practice, the traditional patriarchal attitude is "the less said about mothers, the better." Hal is the prototype of what this attitude can achieve when it works. In the best of all possible patriarchal worlds, mothers would be unnecessary. Hence the explicit fascination with that figment of the male imagination, the man not "of woman born." *The Winter's Tale*, however, insists on motherhood and therefore requires some accommodation to it.

We see the tenuous beginnings of this accommodation when, after Paulina leaves without the baby, Leontes partially relents, as though her departure had activated some area of self-restraint. First, Leontes modifies his response to Paulina: "Whom for this time we pardon" (2.3.173). Second, he changes his approach to the baby: "That thou may commend it strangely to some place / Where chance may nurse or end it" (182–83). The infant's survival hinges on "nursing." Leontes's decree is a metaphor for the capriciousness of maternal nurturance; yet he no longer rules out the possibility of care. This step can thus be regarded as his tentative attempt to test the "nursing" he has so precipitously denied to Mamillius. Although Shakespeare's pastoral ensures that the nature evoked as "some remote and desert place" (176) will be provident, Leontes must do penance, which takes the form of entrusting himself to the care of the woman (Paulina) whom he has previously resisted. There is even a sense in which he had always expected this outcome: "I charg'd thee that she should not come about me: / I knew she would" (43–44). Not only has he been certain that Paulina could be depended on to come after him, perhaps (like Lear) his deepest desire is to be chased and caught by "kind nursery."[6]

The news of Mamillius's death punctures Leontes's delusion (3.2.146–47), as the oracle's announcement does not (140–41), because it carries the jolt of recognition based on the equation of father and son: this death hits home. Leontes's repentance continues this identification through ritual worship of the maternal dyad: "Prithee bring me / To the dead bodies of my queen and son. /

One grave shall be for both" (234–36). It is out of this rejoined symbiotic unit that Leontes will re-create himself: "Once a day I'll visit / The chapel where they lie, and tears shed there / Shall be my recreation" (238–40). His acceptance of Paulina's punishment and guidance provides a living parallel to the buried image: Leontes plays the role of obedient son to mother Paulina, who dictates a period of "fasting" to compensate for the oral deprivation Leontes imposed on Mamillius (211). The play's final scene reenacts the symbiotic unity that Leontes now mourns. Because Hermione lives, Leontes can eventually take the place of the son who has been sacrificed for the father's sacrilege against maternity.

II

The play's ending is earned, but we must ask to what extent Leontes himself earns it and at what cost. That earning is pertinent is shown when, after snapping out of his "bloody thoughts" (3.2.159), Leontes is not allowed to achieve reconciliation simply by announcing it (155–56). Leontes's summary of his errors has omitted, as Paulina's list does not, his two children (190–98). Furthermore, Leontes will be made to mourn for Hermione and thus more rigorously to observe the psychological decorum of atoning for his sin against her. While this repentence is important and necessary, it is not enough. Leontes earns the final resolution only in part. "The play" does much of the earning for him, as witness the immediate shift of geographical location. Leontes might still be mourning ("he shuts himself up" [4.1.19]) were not other rituals wildly performed with which he has nothing to do. A resolution is incubated in the controlled environment of the shepherd's home and then exported to the "real world" of Sicilia where Leontes is now in a condition to accept it.

This resolution addresses the issue of nurturance through the use of oral images. The transition from "things dying" to "things new-born" (3.3.114) is in part accomplished by moving from a negative image of things eaten to a positive vision of things eating. As scapegoat, Antigonus summarizes the play's action to this point by expressing his loss of faith in the baby's "mother" (3.3.17). In recapitulating Leontes's delusion, Antigonus is subjected to the oral chaos to which the delusion has led. Maternal feeding is replaced by the travesty of the hungry bear's "dining on the gentleman" (106), a nightmare version of eating echoed by the ship's going under: "the sea flap-dragon'd it" (98). After the release of the catastrophic natural forces of the bear and the storm, the prospect of the sheep-shearing feast, which is introduced through the clown's inventory of the food he is to buy (4.3.37–49), abruptly restores harmony. The bear exits permanently without the power to threaten a return, which the blatant beast possesses in Book 6 of *The Faerie Queene*. Autolycus as a comic "wolf" can steal to his heart's content and still not disrupt the festivities, so great is the abundance of this new world.

The play turns the generic corner from tragedy to comedy by evoking the joy associated with the season of spring. "Welcome hither, / As is the spring to th' earth" (5.1.151–52), Leontes says as he turns to the "paragon" (153), who proves to be his lost daughter. Spring is particularly welcome after we learn that it is not always forthcoming. Lear must painfully acknowledge the permanent loss of his daughter: "She's dead as earth" (5.3.262). The fulfillment of spring would not be so compelling were it not linked to procreation; this specifically human association is what makes the spring image so powerful and makes us so open to an appeal to "wonder" that needs no explanation. However, the human significance of this spring–birth symbolism is carried entirely by the female characters. The question Sherry Ortner raises—"Is female to male as nature is to culture?"[7]—is pertinent here. On balance, the answer for *The Winter's Tale* is yes because the play represents "great creating Nature" (4.4.88) as women's province.

The indispensable central figure in the sheep-shearing festivity is Perdita, on whom the linked associations of spring, nature, women, procreation, and nurturance converge. As "Flora, / Peering in April's front" (4.4.2–3), she epitomizes the profusion appropriate to this figure as rendered in Botticelli's *Primavera*. Perdita's very survival is a triumph of birth: she is a human "blossom" (3.3.46). As the "mistress of the feast" who "lays it on" (4.3.40), she not only supplies maternal provisions but embodies them. As a rare "piece of beauty" (4.4.32), this "queen of curds and cream" (160) seems naturally to be imaged as food. Though the image is not as explicit for Perdita as for the bride with "Her breast like to a bowle of creame uncrudded" in Spenser's *Epithalamion* (175), her person connotes "innocent milk" (3.2.100).

Perdita serves as the focal point for the recovery of a positive image of the feminine, but the positive image she presents is congenial to patriarchal expectations. Her modesty includes adherence to a political decorum that graciously assumes female subordination. Perdita instinctively accepts the prerogatives of paternal power (4.4.18–24); she readily enters into her socialization as the all-providing female (55–72); she stands for the strict separation of art and nature (82–88), a separation that lends itself to a traditional, polarized view of male and female genders; though she believes in common human denominators, she holds her tongue and declines to challenge Polixenes (443–46); and faced with patriarchal rage, she quickly gives up her "dream" of transcending class hierarchy (447–50). Perdita's demeanor of compliant radiance points the way to the traditional image of woman espoused by the play.

The three women—Hermione, Paulina, and Perdita—are strongly linked with one another. Like the three graces described by Edgar Wind, they seem to have been "unfolded" into three separate characters who can be "infolded"[8] as the facets of a single figure. This figure is the natural bounty imaged by women's bearing and suckling children, as is made clear when Perdita is born. Having been rejected by Leontes, Hermione is forced to withdraw into what becomes a separate female society: "Beseech your Highness, / My women may be with me, for you see / My plight requires it" (2.1.116–18). An impressive female solidarity emerges as Paulina joins mother and newborn daughter as the baby's advocate and symbolic "midwife" (2.3.160). She links gender and nature, in the context of reproduction, by proclaiming: "The office / Becomes a woman best" (2.2.29–30) and "This child was prisoner to the womb, and is / By law and process of great Nature thence / Freed and enfranchis'd" (57–59). Perdita instinctively expresses her allegiance to this female alliance in her defense of a "great creating Nature" (4.4.88).

Each of the women takes on the role of hostess, which is an extension of maternal nurturance. Hermione is "your kind hostess" (1.2.60). Enjoined to "the hostessship" (4.4.72), Perdita is quickly educated into the role of a maternal feeder with a never-ending supply of goods and attentiveness:

> Fie, daughter, when my old wife liv'd, upon
> This day she was both pantler, butler, cook,
> Both dame and servant; welcom'd all, serv'd all;
> Would sing her song, dance her turn; now here,
> At upper end o' th' table, now i' th' middle.
> (55–59)

Even Paulina, who seems least likely to assume the role, conforms to the pattern by becoming a hostess in the final scene, which is held in her "poor house" (5.3.6) where the group "intends to sup" (5.2.103). Of course Paulina has spectacular refreshments to offer, but they are modeled on the original image of maternal nurturance, as Leontes's expression of satisfaction suggests: "O, she's warm! / If this be magic, let it be an art / Lawful as eating" (5.3.109–11). Caring for infants is thus extrapolated to include caring for adult men. While it is better to have men regard women as enablers than as disablers, the final harmony between men and women is based on women's acting as caretakers.

The dramatic principle of *The Winter's Tale* has often been described as a logic of transformation. This transformation is of two kinds: the miraculous change in Leontes as he relinquishes his view of women as degraded and learns to see them as sanctified, and the parallel but less noticed transformation in the women as they shift from threatening to reassuring figures. While the removal of the threat permits the joyous happy ending, it also occasions a loss since the women suffer a contraction of power.

Hermione most vividly illustrates the reductive side effects of the play's logic of transformation. In her first appearance she is vibrant, feisty, and forceful, but once accused of infidelity, she adopts a stance of "patience" (2.1.106), referring herself to "the heavens" (106) and waiting out Leontes's delusion: "The King's will be perform'd!" (115). Hermione's patience (like Desdemona's) would be intolerable were it not that the accused woman is in effect split into two women: Paulina (like Emilia) expresses the angry, active side of the female response to Leontes's outrage. When at last Hermione is revived, her original vitality and vivacity are not recovered. The "feminine" characteristics she incarnates at the end are not the "feminine" qualities she displayed at the outset. She is warm and wrinkled, but she is also thoroughly idealized according to her earlier self-effacing gesture: "This action I now go on / Is for my better grace" (121–22).

Paulina is less of an exception to the general rule of female obedience than she appears to be. Her challenge to Leontes's tyrannical authority is sharp, but it is also limited. Since her anger is in the service of the maternal function, she does not seriously violate the code for appropriate gender behavior. Despite Leontes's accusation that she is a "mankind witch" (2.3.68), she appoints herself to defend Hermione and the infant because "The office / Becomes a woman best" (2.2.29–30). Given Leontes's delusion and Hermione's repression, Paulina's assertive action is justified; moreover, she is clearly working in Leontes's best interests, as he ultimately acknowledges: "Thou canst not speak too much, I have deserv'd / All tongues to talk their bitt'rest" (3.2.215–16). Finally, her domineering role is only temporary. At the end, she removes the mask of punitive and demanding mother, resuming her normal place when she accepts a second marriage, which Leontes arranges for her.

In the last scene Hermione changes from art object to particularized human being as she "descends" and "is stone no more" (5.3.99). Although this rite is important, it is overstressed if we do not also perceive that she remains an icon. If Hermione is a living, directly accessible secular madonna, all the better. Because Hermione's and Leontes's respective roles as all-giving and all-worshiping are fixed, their newly won mutuality is stereotypical. The exchange comprises Hermione's conferring sustenance and forgiveness on Leontes and his conferring appreciative idealization on her. His idolatry, however, needs to be placed in its larger context of patriarchal ideology, for such worship does not prevent Leontes from maintaining social control over female resources.

In good tragic form, Hermione initially suggests that Leontes can never undo the consequences of his deluded accusation: "You scarce can right me throughly, then, to say / You did mistake" (2.1.99–100). The tragic conclusion having been averted, Hermione's surrogate, Paulina, prepares to reward Leontes because he has "paid home" (5.3.4). In *King Lear*, the tension between accountability and forgiveness breaks in favor of the former. Cordelia's "No cause, no cause" is not permitted to withstand the ruthless working out of consequences for which Lear in large part must be held responsible. In *The Winter's Tale*, accountability is superseded and ultimately suspended through the mediation of women: an apparently "free" bounty prevails. Yet the commercial metaphor is still needed to describe the final transaction by which female bounty is extrapolated from the image of maternal nurturance and converted into male bounty, whose circulation is the basis of benevolent patriarchal order.[9] In this sense, the patriarchal body politic is founded on the female body. Hermione blesses her daughter with the nurturance that she had previously been forced to withhold: "You gods, look down / And from your sacred vials pour your graces / Upon my daughter's head" (5.3.121–23). Yet Hermione can no longer claim this nurturant power as her own, attributing it instead to the gods. This displacement impedes the potential female bonding between mother and daughter.[10] Furthermore, the moment is treated as an interlude that leads to patriarchal closure. In the final speech, Leontes returns to the role of dispenser of bounty and director of entertainment.

It may seem that while Leontes retains formal governance, the women have the informal power that really counts. However, that male political control is not merely a formality. The role of Florizel, Polixenes's son, is instructive. He serves, in contrast to Leontes, as a model for an unwavering male faith in women. He is absolute in his commitment to Perdita, to the point of outright violation of patriarchal order. True to his earlier promise—"Or I'll be thine, my fair, / Or not my father's" (4.4.42–43), Florizel renounces his paternal inheritance: "From my succession wipe me, father, I / Am heir to my affection" (480–81). But Florizel's faith is never put to the test because the breach in father–son relations on which patriarchal continuity depends is immediately mended.

In his initial rage at his son's "unfilial" refusal to acknowledge that "The father (all whose joy is nothing else / But fair posterity) should hold some counsel / In such a business" (4.4.406,408–10) as the choice of a bride, Polixenes disowns Florizel: "Whom son I dare not call" (418). But he quickly tempers this extreme position in order to maintain the bond with his son. He makes disinheritance conditional. A kind of patriarchal defense mechanism goes into operation to protect Polixenes's self-interest, deflecting the full force of his anger from Florizel, in whom he has a great investment, to Perdita, who is both female and lower class. Polixenes wants the "divorce" (417) to be between Florizel and the "fresh piece / Of excellent witchcraft" (422–23), "this knack" (428), not between father and son.

While Perdita lapses into fatalism (4.4.474–76), Florizel accepts the guidance of an older man, Camillo, who gently releases Florizel from the either/or thinking on which his defiance of his father is based. Camillo has little difficulty in exposing the youthful "madness" (484) and "desperation" (485) that accompany Florizel's admirable ardor. In place of Florizel's reckless talk—"But as th' unthought-on accident is guilty / To what we wildly do, so we profess / Ourselves to be the slaves of chance, and flies / Of every wind that blows" (538–41), Camillo substitutes "direction" (523). In a series of astute moves, Camillo leads Florizel to accept reconciliation with his father in fiction so that it can later occur in fact. In introducing his "advice" (505) to Florizel, he has already reconnected father and son: "Well, my lord, / If you may please to think I love the King, / And through him what's nearest to him, which is / Your gracious self, embrace" (520-23). Camillo presses this opening further by creating a script through which Florizel internalizes Polixenes: "that he shall not perceive / But that you have your father's bosom there, / And speak his very heart" (562–64). Camillo's plan succeeds even before it is carried out, as is indicated by Florizel's manner of accepting it: "Camillo, / Preserver of my father, now of me, / The medicine of our house" (585–87). This conception of one male "house" to which both father and son belong predicates the resolution that quickly follows. In this patriarchal medicine, Florizel finds "some sap" (565).

The plan involves the reconciliation not only of father and son, but also of the two estranged "best brothers" (1.2.148), Leontes and Polixenes. Camillo's plan envisions "Leontes opening his free arms, and weeping / His welcomes forth; asks thee there, son, forgiveness, / As 'twere i' th' father's person" (4.4.548–50). As the connecting link between Leontes and Polixenes, Camillo preserves the possibility of their friendship. His mediating role is suggested in act 4, scene 2, where men's need for one another is plangently articulated, pulling Camillo in two directions. In a replaying of act 1, scene 2, Polixenes anxiously promises Camillo largesse in an effort to suspend his departure. Again a language of payment and calculation demonstrates the emotional bond: "which if I have not enough consider'd (as too much I cannot), to be more thankful to thee shall be my study, and my profit therein the heaping friendships" (4.2.17–20). But Leontes also needs Camillo: "the penitent King, my master, hath sent for me, to whose feeling sorrows I might be some allay" (6–8). To avoid the new rupture that might result from these ardent, competing claims, Camillo waits until he can "frame" (4.4.509) an enabling fiction that will satisfy both needs at the same time. Once presented with the opportunity to devise this plan, Camillo vividly expresses his longing for Leontes: "Purchase the sight again of dear Sicilia / And that unhappy king, my master, whom / I so much thirst to see" (511–13); and "in whose company / I shall re-view Sicilia, for whose sight / I have a woman's longing" (665–67; "Sicilia" here may be taken as referring to king as well as to country). In the context of the anticipated renewal of male ties, this oral and sex-role imagery can be spoken without embarrassment.

The "miracle" (4.4.534) Camillo performs in restoring patriarchy is a political as well as theatrical feat. The final act of *The Winter's Tale* is organized as a series of reconciliations, of which the Leontes–Hermione reunion—crucial as it is—is only one. As C. L. Barber emphasizes, Leontes's reconciliation with Polixenes precedes the recovery of Hermione.[11] Although the male reconciliations in the first two scenes of act 5 do not complete the play's work, they do suggest how much men achieve through male relationships. The male network is solid and copious enough to supply replacements for Mamillius and Antigonus. Leontes's delusion has resulted in their deaths, but the principle of the identity of "brothers" within the patriarchal system generates adequate substitutes in Florizel (male heir to Leontes) and Camillo (husband for Paulina). Though he subsequently acknowledges Hermione, Leontes expresses at the outset a version of procreation that includes the woman only as the vehicle by which the father's mirror image is produced and that implies male control of reproduction:

> Your mother was most true to wedlock, Prince,
> For she did print your royal father off,
> Conceiving you. Were I but twenty-one,
> Your father's image is so hit in you
> (His very air) that I should call you brother,
> As I did him, and speak of something wildly
> By us perform'd before. Most dearly welcome!
> (5.1.124–30)

This tribute to the strength of male bonds, which make possible the continuity and self-perpetuation of patriarchal order, carries over to the final scene where it coexists with the celebration of Hermione's return. There, the patriarchal background provides both a base of psychological support from which Leontes can venture out to encounter Hermione and a frame to contain the experience.

The informal, domestic power granted to women in this play does not work to their advantage as much as it might appear at first. Their paradoxical position is explained by the compromise intrinsic to their situation: they are a powerful force for transforming the men, yet their power as facilitators is used to reform rather than to transcend the patriarchal framework. Ultimately, their power is efficacious insofar as it is filtered through definitions of women that men find acceptable in the long run. The view that women are central but nonetheless circumscribed properly avoids an overestimation of the role they are allowed. The women's superiority, however dazzling, conforms to the traditional pattern of men's view of women whereby they are either degraded or elevated; a woman is either above or below, but never quite on the same human level (even when she "descends" to it). The elevation of women can be deeply gratifying to men when women can be perceived as using their virtue in men's behalf, placing themselves in the service of men, saving men from their worst selves, and bringing out the best in them. This image of a woman who can be counted on to tutor, rescue, and forgive men is not incompatible with male self-esteem. Leontes's humility, though genuine, is a screen for a male-centered celebration of women.

That Shakespeare's drama centers on male experience and on situations experienced by men may be perfectly natural and obvious, but it also determines the limits of *The Winter's Tale*. First, it eliminates the misleading claims sometimes made in Shakespeare's defense that his mind is androgynous.[12] Second, it clarifies one of the questions that needs to be asked: what are the consequences for *The Winter's Tale* of its male-centeredness? In particular, the view that Leontes achieves a mature masculine identity cannot be maintained without qualification. Patriarchal structures are not merely an exterior formality in this play because their impact is not restricted to state politics but extends to intrafamily politics where they signify the primacy of the male point of view at the deepest emotional levels. The arrangement of familial and sexual roles at the conclusion of *The Winter's Tale* diminishes as well as enhances Leontes's identity. The play sustains the illusion that Leontes can continue to be "boy eternal," now in relation to Hermione, whose maternal standing is indicated by the way Leontes associates her "grace" with "infancy" (5.3.27). His power to manipulate the metaphorical uses of natural female resources (to benevolent ends) has as its negative by-product the imposition of constraints on the possibilities for masculine development. Leontes's capacity to revaluate Hermione's nurturant presence leads to the reformation of his male identity, but the combination of dependence and appropriation in which the revaluation is grounded gives this reformed masculinity built-in limitations.

It is not Shakespeare's express purpose to expose ironically the masculine ideal that Leontes attains in the final scene.[13] On the contrary, Shakespeare does everything in his artistic power to make the conclusion irony-proof and to promote our willing suspension of disbelief. It might be argued that Shakespeare makes the resolution so extravagant or contrived that he forces or invites us to call it into question. But such an argument takes the superficial view of plausibility as verisimilitude and neglects the convincing psychological realism.[14] Theatrical as the ending may be, it is not primarily a witty exercise in metadrama. Such a view presupposes a detachment, which the emotional impact of the ending denies (even after we know the surprise). The normal balance of engagement and detachment described by Maynard Mack[15] is upset here, tilted sharply toward the former. Shakespeare goes out of his way to pull our aesthetic distance up short. Until the final scene, the audience shares Leontes's ignorance, and hence we feel more strongly his subsequent joy. The function of the surrounding humor is not to undercut but to increase the communal spirit of this elation. For example, the responses of the shepherd and clown to their good fortune (5.2.126–74) are less comic relief than comic intensification. To adapt Keats's phrase, the beauty of the comedy here is that it serves not as parody but as "a fine excess."

Shakespeare raises the issues of "suspicion" (5.2.29) and "credit" (62) in order to preempt and disarm skepticism. Likening the dramatic action to "an old tale" (28, 61) enables Shakespeare to capitalize on the difference: "That she is living, / Were it but told you, should be hooted at / Like an old tale; but it appears she lives" (5.3.115–17). The shift from the narrative distance that might permit us to "hoot" to direct experience confronts us with the undeniable, albeit incredible, reality that "she lives." Paulina's stipulation defines the basis of this reality: "It is requir'd / You do awake your faith" (94–95). Shakespeare's faith is awakened too. Precisely because Shakespeare himself is participating in, rather than exposing, this final resolution, it becomes more difficult to gain a perspective for evaluation.

III

I conclude by addressing the larger implications of this account of *The Winter's Tale* for Shakespeare's work as a whole. I am committed to the goal of tracing patterns in Shakespeare's chronological development, but I have tried to complicate our sense of those patterns. In particular, I must dissociate my effort from the suggestion, in T. S. Eliot's classic statement about "the whole pattern formed by the sequence of plays," that the pattern consists in a linear progress toward greater "maturity." Eliot suggests that the late romances have a special status in the overall shape of Shakespeare's career when he observes:

> We can hardly read the later plays attentively without admitting that the father and daughter theme was one of very deep symbolic value to him in his last productive years: Perdita, Marina and Miranda share some beauty of which his earlier heroines do not possess the secret.[16]

And Eliot's own poem "Marina" sanctifies the culminating role played by the late romances in the cumulative body of Shakespeare's work.

However, it is important to question and to qualify the notions of linearity and maturity in Shakespeare's development. From my perspective, *The Winter's Tale* does have a crucial value in the total picture. With regard to relations between men and women, it is more important than *The Tempest* as a point of culmination. Against the background of the destructive antagonism between men and women in the tragedies, the recovery of the possibility for harmonious relations enacted by Leontes and Hermione is miraculous. Nevertheless, *The Winter's Tale* cannot supply a happy ending for Shakespeare's entire corpus. The legitimate need to celebrate the positive aspects of *The Winter's Tale* should not be permitted—because of the pressure of chronological neatness—to obscure the negative elements. I would do justice both to Shakespeare's growth and to his limitations, and I cherish the limitations as a valid, precious part of the cultural tradition we critically transmit.

A complex picture of the fluctuations in the course of Shakespeare's development involves the recognition of loss as well as gain. Specifically, the transition from *Antony and Cleopatra* to *The Winter's Tale* is a retreat as much as an advance. In *Antony and Cleopatra,* even those of us who are sympathetic to Cleopatra's "dream" of "an Emperor Antony" (5.2.76) are forced to acknowledge the reality principle—no matter how paltry we would like to consider it—that qualifies her artful suicide. Although *Antony and Cleopatra* has to answer to the demands of both transcendence and reality, the resolution of *The Winter's Tale* appears not to be pulled in these two directions but to partake of a world made safe for the total fulfillment of transcendence. Yet the concept of patriarchy helps to reveal the reality principle operating at the end of *The Winter's Tale.*

Cleopatra and Hermione both preside over a conclusion that consists in the woman's giving herself completely. But although *Antony and Cleopatra* may give us "new heaven," *The Winter's Tale* gives us "new earth," creating a real world fully conducive to transcendence, a world in which the logic of transformation proceeds unimpeded to the total fulfillment lacking in the earlier play. The rite that Paulina arranges in the last scene of *The Winter's Tale* celebrates the nurturant life that Cleopatra in her final performance is forced to relinquish. In seeking the "fire and air" of an imaginary heaven and in relinquishing her "other elements" to "baser life" (5.2.289,290), Cleopatra renounces what *The Winter's Tale* calls "Dear life" (5.3.103). The "Dear life" that "redeems" Hermione includes an actual family. The absent Antony and the asp, however intensely imagined as "husband" and "baby," cannot compare with Leontes and Perdita, who are present to receive Hermione's life-giving "blessing."

However, it would be incorrect to end on an exclusively optimistic note. The contrast between the two plays is not so one-sided. The gains in fulfillment in *The Winter's Tale* are achieved at a cost—the imposition of restrictive definitions of gender. To attain the climactic harmony of *The Winter's Tale*, Shakespeare retreats from the experiment in heterosexual androgyny in *Antony and Cleopatra* and returns to a traditional conception of polarized sexual roles. The mutuality between men and women dramatized in *The Winter's Tale* is schematic compared with the vibrant (though troubled) give-and-take enacted by Antony and Cleopatra. The contrast between the tragedies and the late romances is relative rather than absolute. The romances continue in a different form the exploration of tragic motives, and the late plays remain stubbornly problematic.

Notes

PREFACE

1. Raymond Williams, *The Long Revolution* (London: Chatto & Windus, 1961), p. 48. Also useful is Williams's observation on critical method:

> We have got into the habit, since we realized how deeply works or values could be determined by the whole situation in which they are expressed, of asking about these relationships in a standard form: "what is the relation of this art to this society?" But "society," in this question, is a specious whole. If the art is part of the society, there is no solid whole, outside it, to which, by the form of our question, we concede priority.
>
> (p. 45)

2. Lawrence Stone, "The Rise of the Nuclear Family in Early Modern England: The Patriarchal Stage," in *The Family in History*, ed. Charles E. Rosenberg (Philadelphia: University of Pennsylvania Press, 1975), p. 34. Stone, however, lacks a sociology of the theater. Commenting on the shift from the parish to the familial household, he remarks:

> Even traditional parochial festival and carnival organizations died away under the withering blast of Puritan disapproval of such pagan relics as maypoles and church-ales. . . . [The parish's] social, festive, psychological and religious functions tended to be replaced by the household.
>
> (p. 29)

This account omits the communal, festive role of popular commercial theater that C. L. Barber reconstructs in *Shakespeare's Festive Comedy* (Princeton: Princeton University Press, 1959). Perhaps a two-way interdisciplinary exchange in which Shakespeare studies can contribute to Stone's historical picture, as well as learn from it, is in order. One assessment of Stone's work from a Shakespearean standpoint is Marianne Novy's "Shakespeare and Emotional Distance in the Elizabethan Family," *Theater Journal* 33 (1981): 316–26. For suggestive discussions of Shakespeare's theater as a social institution, see Louis Adrian Montrose, "The Purpose of Playing: Reflections on a Shakespearean Anthropology," *Helios*, n.s., 7 (1980): 51–74; and Stephen J. Greenblatt's concluding commentary on *1 Henry IV* in "Invisible Bullets: Renaissance Authority and Its Subversion," in *Shakespeare's "Rough Magic": Essays in Honor of C. L. Barber*, ed. Peter Erickson and Coppélia Kahn (Newark, Del.: University of Delaware Press, 1985).

    3. Stone, "Rise of the Nuclear Family," pp. 54–55.

    4. In *New Bearings in English Poetry* (London: Chatto & Windus, 1932), F. R. Leavis advocates the realignment by which "Donne comes to be associated with Shakespeare in contrast to Spenser and Milton" (p. 8); and in *Revaluation* (London: Chatto & Windus, 1936), Leavis contrasts "the line of wit" with the tradition of Spenser, Milton, Keats, and Tennyson, condemning "the spirit of Spenser" as "incantatory, remote from speech" (p. 56).

INTRODUCTION

    1. Leslie Fiedler, the critic most prominently associated with this theme, discusses it in *The Stranger in Shakespeare* (New York: Stein & Day, 1972), a book that grew out of Fiedler's brief commentary on Shakespeare in *Love and Death in the American Novel* (New York: Criterion Books, 1960), pp. 24–26. But a renewed interest in male bonds and their effect on heterosexual ties has emerged recently, in the work of Shirley Garner and Louis Adrian Montrose (cited in note 5 below) and notably in Janet Adelman's comprehensive analysis, "Male Bonding in Shakespeare's Comedies," originally presented at the 1979 Modern Language Association convention and published in *Shakespeare's "Rough Magic": Essays in Honor of C. L. Barber*, ed. Peter Erickson and Coppélia Kahn (Newark, Del.: University of Delaware Press, 1985).

    2. For an extended discussion of Shakespeare's authorial role, see my essay "Shakespeare and the 'Author-Function,' " in *Shakespeare's "Rough Magic."*

    3. The historian Joan Kelly-Gadol formulated this contradiction in her remarks at the Berkshire Conference on Women's History, Mount Holyoke College, August 1978. She discusses the ways the Renaissance affected men and women differently in her essay "Did Women Have a Renaissance?" in *Becoming Visible: Women in European History*, ed. Renate Bridenthal and

Claudia Koontz (Boston: Houghton Mifflin, 1977), pp. 137–64. See also the reference to the Renaissance in her section on historical periodization in her theoretical essay "The Social Relation of the Sexes: Methodological Implications of Women's History," *Signs* 1 (1975–76): 811.

4. Even here, however, Janet Adelman argues that the male tie is "more significant as an expression of Coriolanus's need for a mirror image of himself than as the expression of his homosexual desire," in " 'Anger's My Meat': Feeding, Dependency, and Aggression in *Coriolanus*," in *Representing Shakespeare: New Psychoanalytic Essays*, ed. Murray M. Schwartz and Coppélia Kahn (Baltimore: Johns Hopkins University Press, 1980), p. 149, n. 25. Adelman tellingly relates the Coriolanus–Aufidius bond to the play's network of oral imagery:

> Here, far from Rome, Coriolanus at last allows his hunger and his vulnerability to be felt, and he is given food. He presents himself to Aufidius during a great feast. . . . here in Antium, the play moves toward a fantasy in which nourishment may be safely taken because it is given by a male, by a father-brother-twin rather than a mother.
>
> (p. 139)

5. Shirley Garner discusses the dissolution of the Helena–Hermia bond as a prerequisite to male control in "*A Midsummer Night's Dream:* 'Jack shall have Jill; / Nought shall go ill,' " *Women's Studies* 9 (1981): 47–63. Louis Adrian Montrose gives a related account in "The Cult of Elizabeth and the Sexual Politics of *A Midsummer Night's Dream*," presented at the conference on Renaissance Woman/Renaissance Man, Yale University, March 1982. Montrose shows that despite Elizabeth's power and the literary cult celebrating it, Shakespeare's play exhibits a fundamental patriarchal bias.

6. In "Doubling, Women's Anger, and Genre," *Women's Studies* 9 (1982): 107–19, Marilyn L. Williamson argues that Shakespeare defuses the potential power of female bonds by creating pairs of women who are divided by social class. The lower-class woman can protest on behalf of her higher-status companion, but the latter's modesty preserves intact the conventional ideal of the good woman who does not threaten male domination. The latter's image prevails over the former's temporary explosion, thus containing it.

See also Virginia Woolf's comment in *A Room of One's Own* (1929) (New York: Harcourt, Brace & World, 1957):

> Cleopatra did not like Octavia. And how completely *Antony and Cleopatra* would have been altered had she done so! . . . Cleopatra's

> only feeling about Octavia is one of jealousy. Is she taller than I am? How does she do her hair? The play, perhaps, required no more. But how interesting it would have been if the relationship between the two women had been more complicated. . . . So much has been left out, unattempted.
>
> (p. 86)

Toni A. H. McNaron's unpublished essay "Female Bonding in Shakespeare: Its Absence and Presence," which I read after completing my own discussion of male versus female bonding, shows how much has been "left out, unattempted." Of Lear's daughters, McNaron notes: "I sometimes feel that, rather than having a dead or absent mother, these three never had a mother at all." Motherless women are deprived of the original female bond, the mother–daughter tie, and thus cannot perform the function, indispensable to identity, that Woolf calls "think[ing] back through her mothers" (p. 101).

7. Eugene Waith, "Manhood and Valor in Two Shakespearean Tragedies," *English Literary History* 17 (1950): 262–73. A similar distinction between narrow and inclusive versions of masculinity is explored in Robert B. Heilman's "Manliness in the Tragedies: Dramatic Variations," in *Shakespeare: 1564–1964*, ed. Edward A. Bloom (Providence, R. I.: Brown University Press, 1964), pp. 19-37.

1. SEXUAL POLITICS AND SOCIAL STRUCTURE IN *AS YOU LIKE IT*

1. I borrow this phrase from T. S. Eliot's essay "Andrew Marvell" (1921), in *Selected Essays: 1917–1932* (New York: Harcourt, Brace, 1932), p. 252. My essay on *As You Like It*, which forms the basis of this chapter, was presented at the 1979 Modern Language Association convention at the session on "Marriage and the Family in Shakespeare," where I received valuable commentary from Shirley Garner and Carol Neely, chair and respondent, respectively, for the session. After completing my work on the play, I discovered Louis Adrian Montrose's " 'The Place of a Brother' in *As You Like It:* Social Process and Comic Form," *Shakespeare Quarterly* 32 (1981): 28–54, whose approach I regard as complementary to my own.

2. Recent studies by Marilyn French and Linda Bamber suffer from a tendency to invest too much energy in abstract definitions of genre categories, as though Shakespeare managed each genre as a strictly separate Platonic form, and too little energy in close interpretation of individual variations. In *Shake-*

speare's Division of Experience (New York: Simon & Schuster, 1981), French pursues her thesis that each genre has its own gender to a formulaic, literalistic extreme, as I have noted in my review of her study in *Women's Studies* 9 (1982): 189–201. Bamber's *Comic Women, Tragic Men: A Study of Gender and Genre in Shakespeare* (Stanford: Stanford University Press, 1982) is far more subtle but nonetheless echoes French's project in stressing a rigid generic division in Shakespeare's artistic labor. Bamber's brief discussion of comedy (Ch. 5) creates intrageneric difficulty because she overrides differences among individual plays in her effort to assimilate them to a common mold, while intergenerically she emphasizes differences at the expense of continuities. For a full discussion of Bamber's approach, see my review of her book in *Women's Studies* 10 (1984): 342–49.

3. I find unconvincing C. L. Barber's argument in *Shakespeare's Festive Comedy* (Princeton: Princeton University Press, 1959) that the songs convey the missing positive note: "They provide for the conclusion of the comedy what marriage usually provides: an expression of the going-on power of life" (p. 118). Barber works too hard to create this festive closure, overstating the affirmation produced by the songs while glossing over the full force of the discomfort caused by the lack of marriage among the central characters. I draw attention to my disagreement here because it illustrates in microcosm my departure from Barber's use of festive comic form. Although he distinguishes the two phases of "release" and "clarification," Barber's practice nonetheless blurs them because the final communal celebration of "the going-on power of life" retains a wishful element characteristic of the earlier stage of festive release. The result is often to make the comic clarification more genial than the evidence warrants. My experience of *As You Like It* differs from Barber's because I see the reality that qualifies and places festivity as a more stringent one. The "resistance" (p. 88) or "tension" (p. 224) against which the festive release pushes off frequently returns in a new, more subtle form in the final moment of clarification, one major source of this renewed tension being relations between men and women and the social structure that organizes them. Yet, as the present chapter makes clear, it is Barber's comic paradigm itself that has made me see these plays differently. I am heavily indebted to the festive concept of dramatic action, but I modify it in order to be more responsive to the gap between ideal festive expectations and actual result. What makes Shakespeare's comic endings compelling is their dramatization of this gap, however muted, rather than of simple fulfillment.

Thus, for example, the songs that conclude *Love's Labor's Lost*, while aiming to invoke the resources of festivity, in fact contribute to the overall mood of thwarted festivity.

4. Barber's formulation for this movement in *Shakespeare's Festive Comedy* is "through release to clarification" (p. 6). In "The Argument of Comedy" (in *English Institute Essays, 1948*, ed. D. A. Robertson, Jr. [New York: Columbia University Press, 1949], pp. 58–73), Northrop Frye uses Keats's "green world" (*Endymion*, I, 16) to describe the middle phase, which mediates between an obstructionist society dominated by people "who are helplessly driven by ruling passions, neurotic compulsions" (p. 61) and "a new social unit" (p. 60) that conveys "the birth of a renewed sense of social integration" (p. 61). This comic structure is elaborated in Frye's *A Natural Perspective: The Development of Shakespearean Comedy and Romance* (New York: Columbia University Press, 1965), pp. 73–79.

5. In "The Failure of Relationship Between Men and Women in *Love's Labor's Lost*," *Women's Studies* 9 (1981): 65–81, I show how the men's poems appeal to conventions of female domination and male humility in love poetry and how these conventions shape the dramatic action, creating a fixed barrier that blocks love.

6. See Clara Park, "As We Like It: How a Girl Can Be Smart and Still Popular," *American Scholar* 42 (1973): 262–78; reprinted in *The Woman's Part: Feminist Criticism of Shakespeare*, ed. Carolyn Ruth Swift Lenz, Gayle Greene, and Carol Thomas Neely (Urbana: University of Illinois Press, 1980), pp. 100–16.

7. Norman O. Brown employs this passage in his own celebration of the horn: "Metamorphoses II: Actaeon," *American Poetry Review* 1 (1972): 38–40.

8. Barber, *Festive Comedy*, p. 10.

9. Adrienne Rich provides a critique of the conservative use of the concept *androgyny* and a summary of recent writing on the subject in *Of Woman Born: Motherhood as Experience and Institution* (New York: W. W. Norton, 1976), pp. 62–63. Rich's poem "The Stranger," in *Diving into the Wreck* (New York: W. W. Norton, 1973), declares proudly: "I am the androgyne" (p. 19). But the revaluation of androgyny in her prose work leads Rich to disavow the term in "Natural Resources," in *The Dream of a Common Language* (New York: W. W. Norton, 1978): "There are words I cannot choose again: / *humanism androgyny*" (p. 66).

10. I do not mean to suggest that this is a positive ending in

the sense of being the best possible outcome, but the women's continued assertion of independence is a valid response to the less-than-ideal circumstances with which they must deal. It allows them to retain their integrity—an alternative preferable to capitulation.

11. In Anne Barton's judgment, *As You Like It* "stands as the fullest and most stable realization of Shakespearean comic form" (" 'As You Like It' and 'Twelfth Night': Shakespeare's Sense of an Ending," in *Shakespearean Comedy: Stratford-Upon-Avon Studies 14,* ed. Malcolm Bradbury and David Palmer [New York: Crane, Russak & Co., 1972], p. 161). Barton speaks of Shakespeare's loss of "faith" in comic endings after the perfection of *As You Like It* and of the "renewed faith" made possible by his "readjustment of form" in the late romances (pp. 179–80). Both the loss and the recovery of faith involve Shakespeare's changing attitudes toward the viability of benign patriarchy. In particular, *The Winter's Tale* restores this faith (after its shattering in the tragedies) by reestablishing patriarchal harmony in a believable form.

12. In this regard *The Merchant of Venice* offers a useful contrast. The conclusion of *Love's Labor's Lost* presents a three-way stalemate. Marital bonds, male bonds, and female bonds are all sources of vague discomfort: none can be affirmed. *As You Like It* affirms marriage by strengthening male bonds and eliminating female bonds. *The Merchant of Venice* breaks the stalemate in a different way. Marriage is achieved by disrupting the bond between Antonio and Bassanio, but the alliance between Portia and Nerissa remains in effect, as their comparatively sharp deployment of the cuckold motif attests. The source of uneasiness in *The Merchant of Venice*, however, is Portia's defeat of a Jewish father in the earlier court scene and, in particular, her problematic speech about Christian bounty (4.1.184–202), problematic partly because her own behavior toward Shylock fails to exhibit the mercy she recommends to him.

13. For an example of this contrast between comedies and histories, see R. J. Dorius, "Shakespeare's Dramatic Modes and *Antony and Cleopatra*" in *Literatur als Kritik des Lebens: Festschrift zum 65. Geburtstag von Ludwig Borinski* (Heidelberg: Quelle & Meyer, 1975), pp. 83–96. Dorius's overview is useful but overdrawn in the way I have suggested.

14. The use of "motherless man" is from Leslie Fiedler's discussion of Shakespeare in *Love and Death in the American Novel* (New York: Criterion Books, 1960), p. 26.

15. The existence of a need to avoid mothers can be demon-

strated by two subsequent plays, *All's Well That Ends Well* and *Measure for Measure.* Both plays, in explicitly confronting procreation, testify to the difficulty of assimilating it. Part of the reason they are problem plays is the unresolved ambivalence about the sexuality evidenced in the pregnancies of Helena and Juliet. However necessary procreation is acknowledged to be in theory, its actual practice is often in Shakespeare made to appear suspect, troubling, or forbidding, as Venus's argument for procreation illustrates (*Venus and Adonis,* 168). In *The Comedy of Errors* at the beginning of Shakespeare's career, birth is evoked in passing in an equivocal, infelicitous line as "The pleasing punishment that women bear" (1.1.46); not until *Pericles,* in the final phase of Shakespeare's career, is procreation dignified, its integrity persuasively dramatized. And not until *The Winter's Tale* does he begin to approach the reconciliation of art and procreation hypothesized in sonnets 15–17.

16. Frye, "Argument of Comedy," p. 69.

2. FATHERS, SONS, AND BROTHERS IN *HENRY V*

1. Examples of the latter category are those who accept the description of the play as a patriotic celebration and find it a lapse in Shakespeare's usual acumen, critics such as A. P. Rossiter and Sigurd Burckhardt. In "Ambivalence: The Dialectic of the Histories," in *Angel with Horns,* ed. Graham Storey (London: Longmans, Green & Co., 1961), Rossiter depicts *Henry V* simply as "a propaganda-play on National Unity: heavily orchestrated for the brass. The sounding—and very impressive—Rhetoric shows how something is being stifled. The wartime-values demand a determined 'one-eyedness' " (pp. 57–58). Though his discussion is much more complicated, Burckhardt finds the play conforming to a similar patriotic model, resulting in the same constriction. In " 'Swoll'n with Some Other Grief': Shakespeare's Prince Hal Trilogy," in his *Shakespearean Meanings* (Princeton: Princeton University Press, 1968), Burckhardt characterizes Shakespeare's action in *Henry V* as "withdrawal" (p. 196): "Shakespeare takes a rest . . . and knowingly chooses a partial and partisan clarity" (p. 193). In this play, Shakespeare "refuses" the "responsibility" of the "true dramatist"—"that of making a world" (p. 190). He "surrenders his claim to 'authorship': 'Take it, God, / For it is none but thine!' " (p. 195). A more profitable starting point for interpretation may be the work of critics who respond positively to the alleged epic status of *Henry V.* The unabashed enthusiasm of J. Dover Wilson and

J. H. Walter has the merit of pointing the way out of a wholly static image of the play. Wilson's defense is based on his view that Henry V changes and deepens during the course of the drama: "But a shift in focus there certainly is, and it is one that might well have been adopted by a dramatist who set out to inflame an audience, prone to admire one kind of hero, with worship for another kind altogether" (Introduction, *King Henry V* [Cambridge: Cambridge University Press, 1947], p. xxv). Walter, following Wilson, emphasizes "the unfolding of Henry's character" (Introduction to the Arden edition, *King Henry V* [London: Methuen, 1954], p. xxxiii). Though I differ with Wilson's and Walter's conclusions, their approach rightly acknowledges Henry V's development within the play. Such development suggests that close reading is no less pertinent here than for any other of Shakespeare's plays, whereas disappointment in *Henry V* tends to justify inattention to the language that confirms the original disappointment.

2. In a previous essay, " 'The fault / My father made': The Anxious Pursuit of Heroic Fame in Shakespeare's *Henry V*," *Modern Language Studies* 10 (1979–80): 10–25, I have given a detailed analysis of the play's language and overall dramatic structure. This chapter is based on a second essay, "Fathers, Sons, and Brothers: *Henry V* as a Culmination of the Second Tetralogy and as a Prelude to *Hamlet*," presented at the Shakespeare Association of America meeting in San Francisco in 1979.

3. W. B. Yeats's account in "At Stratford-on-Avon" (1901), in *Essays and Introductions* (New York: Macmillan, 1961), pp. 96–110, has fixed in our minds the false image of Henry V as cold, tough, and impersonal when Yeats scornfully calls him "that ripened Fortinbras" (p. 108), whereas Richard II is "that unripened Hamlet" (p. 108). Yeats defines "Shakespeare's myth" (p. 107) as a conflict between the two types represented by Richard II, "the vessel of porcelain" (p. 108), and Henry V, "the vessel of clay" (p. 108). With all Yeats's sympathy skewed toward Richard II, Henry V is demoted to the category of "an empty man who thrust him from his place, and saw all that could be seen from very emptiness" (p. 107). This overdrawn contrast prevents Yeats from listening to the troubled undertone of Henry V's language and from hearing the substantial core of tenderness and pity that dilutes his masculine toughness. Belatedly, Yeats makes the observation that "everybody talks of him as if he succeeded, although he fails in the end, as all men great and little fail in Shakespeare" (p. 108) and that Shakespeare "spoke his tale, as he spoke all tales, with tragic irony" (p. 109).

But Yeats fails to integrate this perception into his overall interpretation of *Henry V*, and he refuses to acknowledge the sympathy for Henry V that "tragic irony" might permit.

4. Ernst Kris, "Prince Hal's Conflict" (1948), in his *Psychoanalytic Explorations in Art* (1952) (New York: Schocken Books, 1964), p. 285.

5. Ibid, p. 286.

6. Norman O. Brown, "Rome—A Psychoanalytic Study," *Arethusa* 7 (1974): 97.

7. Kris comments: "Summoned to battle, the King kneels in prayer in which he disclaims any complicity in his father's crime; thus prepared, the hero can conquer" ("Prince Hal's Conflict," p. 284). The problem with this approach is that the king's attempted preparation does not work. The act of disclaiming is not enough, and the remainder of the scene suggests that the new king cannot shake his "complicity in his father's crime."

8. Wilson, Introduction, *King Henry V*, p. xli.

9. Kris remarks that the conflict between "impulse and inhibition" is "fully resolved only when from moral scrutiny Henry proceeds to heroic venture, when as a leader of men who are determined to fight with a clear conscience against overwhelming odds, he feels himself one among peers." ("Prince Hal's Conflict," p. 285). Kris's "clear conscience" begs the question whether or not this "clear conscience" has been earned. At this point in the play, Kris ceases to examine the text, and his "fully resolved" adds psychoanalytic support to the general idea of Henry V's dazzling success. Yet Shakespeare's dramatization continues to show, underneath the tide of heroic euphoria, "the means / How things are perfected" (*H5*, 1.1.68–69).

10. In *Henry V*, Shakespeare criticizes a male fantasy whereas in *As You Like It* he participates in male wish-fulfillment. In determining the degree of Shakespeare's critical distance from, or his uncritical involvement in, patriarchal structures within the plays, it is necessary to proceed on a case-by-case basis: there is no single answer that fits every instance. A comparative perspective is useful for indicating Shakespeare's relative disengagement in *Henry V* from his complacency toward male gratification in *As You Like It*.

11. The sequence in *1 Henry VI* that ends in the analogous double death of Talbot and his son provides an illuminating comparison with act 4, scene 6 of *Henry V*:

Thou antic Death, which laugh'st us here to scorn,
Anon, from thy insulting tyranny,
Coupled in bonds of perpetuity,
Two Talbots, winged through the lither sky,
In thy despite shall scape mortality.

(*1H6*, 4.7.18–22)

Both episodes are romanticized versions of immortal fame, but they are not romantic in the same way. The difference is that the narrative frame brackets the York–Suffolk scene as a much more conspicuous epitome. The York–Suffolk apotheosis as elaborated by Shakespeare has no precedent in his sources; it is as though Shakespeare invents it to show how chronicle can be spontaneously generated by chivalric sentimentality.

12. A. R. Myers, *England in the Late Middle Ages* (1952) (Baltimore: Penguin Books, 1971), p. 11. See also Lawrence Stone's summary in "The Rise of the Nuclear Family in Early Modern England: The Patriarchal Stage," in *The Family in History*, ed. Charles E. Rosenberg (Philadelphia: University of Pennsylvania Press, 1975):

> The landed classes of the late fifteenth and early sixteenth centuries underwent a severe crisis of confidence: their medieval military functions were eroded, but nothing else was available to take the place of these functions. . . . They first threw themselves into a romantic revival of the ancient chivalric ideal, but that was too brittle to sustain the weight placed upon it, and it soon collapsed.
>
> (p. 35)

Context must be taken into account in reading Canterbury's oration in the "great-chain-of-being" vein (*H5*, 1.2.183–214). The archbishop is not simply announcing his belief in an ideal of political order; more accurately, he is using the inflated rhetoric of this ideal for his own ulterior ends. A straightforward Tillyardian interpretation thus misses the mark. In *The Crisis of the Aristocracy: 1558–1641*, abridged ed. (New York: Oxford University Press, 1967), Lawrence Stone, who cites (p. 15) the cornerstone of E. M. W. Tillyard's *Elizabethan World Picture* (London: Chatto & Windus, 1943)—Ulysses's speech on "degree"—has usefully demonstrated the need to see metaphysical statements in their social context, to see the tension between Elizabethan professions of belief and actual practice. Shakespeare's later history plays enact this tension. Similarly, we should not take the York–Suffolk set piece at face value. In the chapters "Achilles Hero" and "Our Virgil" of his *Hero and Saint: Shakespeare and the Graeco-Roman He-*

roic Tradition (New York: Oxford University Press, 1971), Reuben A. Brower develops a literary historical contrast between the Homeric Achilles and the Virgilian Aeneas that provides a useful framework for Henry V's conflicting impulses: he conscientiously adheres to an Aeneas-like model of moral compunction while at the same time he is tempted to affect an Achilles-like stress on martial action in which *pietas* might be inoperative.

13. One small piece of "subtextual" evidence for filial hostility is the fact that Alexander "killed his best friend, Clytus" (*H5*, 4.7.38–39) because the latter praised Alexander's father. J. H. Walter notes in his introduction to the Arden edition of *King Henry V:* "Alexander became heated with wine and boastful of his achievements and scornful of those of his father, Philip. Cleitus, also heated with wine, praised Philip and recklessly taunted Alexander" (p. 125).

14. The sexual convention involved here is akin to the one Madelon Gohlke finds in Theseus's putatively festive remarks to Hippolyta at the opening of *A Midsummer Night's Dream*, as elucidated in " 'I wooed thee with my sword': Shakespeare's Tragic Paradigms," in *Representing Shakespeare: New Psychoanalytic Essays*, ed. Murray M. Schwartz and Coppélia Kahn (Baltimore: Johns Hopkins University Press, 1980), pp. 170–87. See also Gohlke's critique of Denis de Rougement's handling of the love-as-war metaphor (p. 182).

15. Coppélia Kahn, *Man's Estate: Masculine Identity in Shakespeare* (Berkeley: University of California Press, 1981), p. 72.

16. A comparison between Tamburlaine's approach to Zenocrate and Henry V's to Katherine is instructive. In both instances, the presence of a woman establishes limits to omnivorous heroism; but whereas Tamburlaine is inspired to worshipful reverence, Henry V engages in aggressive wit.

17. Following Yeats's 1901 essay, "At Stratford-on-Avon," Harley Granville-Barker remarks: "And where now is that fine upstanding gentleman, Henry V? He is still at hand, and still commands our unreserved admiration. But his name is Fortinbras" ("From *Henry V* to *Hamlet*" (1925), in *More Prefaces to Shakespeare* [Princeton: Princeton University Press, 1974], pp. 149–50). Granville-Barker argues that *Henry V* marks the beginning of an "artistic crisis through which Shakespeare passed" (p. 143), but only because the play is a "dead end" (p. 137) that teaches its author a negative lesson: "For behind the action, be the play farce or tragedy, there must be some spiritually significant idea, or it will hang lifeless. And this is what is lacking in

Henry V" (p. 146). Granville-Barker's approach leads to an absolute contrast between *Henry V* as the "danger-point" (p. 148) and *Hamlet* as the "crowning achievement" (p. 149). I reject Granville-Barker's simplistic, negative view of *Henry V* and see the play as a more positive prelude to *Hamlet*.

18. In *Shakespeare and the Problem of Meaning* (Chicago: University of Chicago Press, 1981), Norman Rabkin makes a similar point about the centrality of *Henry V* in Shakespeare's work as a whole when he argues that the play's "irreducible complexity" brings Shakespeare "to a point of crisis," initiating "a spiritual struggle in Shakespeare that he would spend the rest of his career working through" (pp. 61–62). "*Henry V* is too good a play for criticism to go on calling it a failure" (p. 59).

19. See my discussion of the story motif in " 'The fault / My father made': The Anxious Pursuit of Heroic Fame in Shakespeare's *Henry V*," *Modern Language Studies* 10 (1979–1980): 10–25, especially pp. 17–18. The problem of validating identity through story is graphically clear because of the chorus's false appeal to simple repetition of the preexisting story: "Vouchsafe to those that have not read the story / That I may prompt them" (5.Cho.1–2).

3. MATERNAL IMAGES AND MALE BONDS IN *HAMLET, OTHELLO,* AND *KING LEAR*

1. The emphatic quality of Hamlet's declaration is reinforced by the iteration: "In my heart's core, ay, in my heart of heart" (3.2.73). Harold Jenkins notes in the Arden edition of *Hamlet* (London: Methuen, 1982): "Both phrases mean the same, on the supposed etymology of 'core,' from L. 'cor': in the very centre of my heart" (p. 292).

2. David Leverenz gives a useful analysis of the ghost's rhetoric in his essay "The Woman in Hamlet: An Interpersonal View," in *Representing Shakespeare: New Psychoanalytic Essays*, ed. Murray M. Schwartz and Coppélia Kahn (Baltimore: Johns Hopkins University Press, 1980), pp. 110–28. In addition, it should be noted that the ghost's manipulative, guilt-inducing appeals to Hamlet's love in act 1, scene 5 have their parallel in Henry IV's style of taunting overstatement in his private audiences with Hal (*1H4*, 3.2; *2H4*, 4.5).

3. In *Shakespeare's Development and the Problem Comedies* (Berkeley: University of California Press, 1981), Richard P. Wheeler nicely observes that Hamlet's impulse to resist the ghost is not in

the first instance a question of moral correctness but rather a matter of instinctive psychological self-defense:

> Hamlet struggles against his own declared intention at a level deeper than his will and in a way not entirely explained by fear of repressed motives. He involuntarily seeks to preserve the potential integrity of self violated by his own attempt to take in and identify totally with the image of his father embodied in the ghost's command. This psychological resistance is analogous to the expulsion reaction in the biochemistry of an organism, set into action by the intrusion of alien tissues. Hamlet tries to perform a kind of self-transplant upon his own person, and the core of his individual self will not accept the foreign intruder.

(p. 194)

4. This position is exemplified by Harold C. Goddard's chapter on the play in vol. 1 of *The Meaning of Shakespeare*, 2 vols. (Chicago: University of Chicago Press, 1951). Goddard argues that Hamlet's invocation of "a divinity that shapes our ends" (5.2.10) strikes an absolutely false note that merely sugars over his murder of Rosencrantz and Guildenstern. Yet, despite Hamlet's use of divinity blithely to excuse his "conscience" (5.2.58), this image of divinity does not merely signal Hamlet's surrender to the ghost. The "divinity that shapes our ends" and the "special providence" (219–20) are different from the ghost because they signify his positive use of the *contemptus mundi* tradition in the graveyard. Much as we may regret the necessity of Hamlet's availing himself of it "betimes" (224), this cultural resource is an expression not simply of despair and resignation, but rather of a vital insight about mortality that gives Hamlet a larger perspective on "monarchs and outstretch'd heroes" (2.2.263–64) such as Alexander (5.1.197–212), "Imperious Caesar" (213–16), and even perhaps his majestical father. Nor does Hamlet passively submit to the shaping force of the divinity, as Goddard claims. Hamlet actively shapes his end, an end that includes a new power to shape language and to construct male bonds that enable forgiveness.

5. As *Hamlet* dramatizes, men's sharply divided view of women as either chaste or sullied may be traced to a maternal base: behind the extremes of good and bad women lie the ideal and terrible mothers. Dorothy Dinnerstein's *The Mermaid and the Minotaur: Sexual Arrangements and Human Malaise* (New York: Harper & Row, 1976) and Nancy Chodorow's *The Reproduction of Mothering: Psychoanalysis and the Sociology of Gender* (Berkeley: University of California Press, 1978) portray the male's divided view of women as activated by asymmetrical parenting, in which the

mother is exclusively responsible for child rearing, thus the son's dependency on the mother for total satisfaction and trust and concommitantly his anxiety about total betrayal and separation. This initial relationship becomes the model by which subsequent women are experienced in the extreme terms of good mother or terrible mother, or an oscillation between the two. However, Adrienne Rich criticized the Dinnerstein-Chodorow analysis in "Motherhood: The Contemporary Emergency and the Quantum Leap" (1978), in *On Lies, Secrets, and Silence* (New York: W. W. Norton, 1979), pp. 259–73 and—more sharply—in "Compulsory Heterosexuality and Lesbian Existence," *Signs* 5 (1980): 631–60. Rich argues that male involvement in child rearing would be inadequte to eliminate misogyny as a social force. In Rich's view, Dinnerstein and Chodorow underestimate the problem and vastly overestimate the efficacy of their solution.

6. According to T. S. Eliot's logic in "Hamlet and His Problems" (1919), in *Selected Essays: 1917–1932* (New York: Harcourt, Brace, 1932), 121–26, Gertrude is too small an object to account for the magnitude of the emotion Hamlet expends in relation to her; therefore, his emotion must refer to something else that we can never discover. But, in encouraging the search for a more "objective correlative" to replace Gertrude, Eliot diverts us from one of the direct causes of Hamlet's alienation. The play makes clear that the human family—" 'With blood of fathers, mothers, daughters, sons' " (2.2.458)—is Hamlet's "cue for passion" (561), and in particular, as the image of Hecuba attests, his mother is one focus of his emotional distress. A useful antidote to Eliot's essay is Rebecca Smith's "A Heart Cleft in Twain: The Dilemma of Shakespeare's Gertrude," in *The Woman's Part: Feminist Criticism of Shakespeare,* ed. Carolyn Ruth Swift Lenz, Gayle Greene, and Carol Thomas Neely (Urbana: University of Illinois Press, 1980), pp. 194–210. Smith suggests that the way to approach the "excess" that troubled Eliot is to show how the disparity between Hamlet's view of his mother and Gertrude's own self-image contributes to our understanding of Hamlet's needs rather than to Shakespeare's "artistic failure." The predominance of the male hero creates a situation in which the male is the perceiver and the woman is the perceived: images of women cannot therefore be read as objective types but to a significant degree must be treated as products of the male psyche.

7. This imagery is developed in *Macbeth* where Lady Macbeth literalizes her metaphor "the milk of human kindness" (1.5.17) by attempting to turn the "milk" in "my woman's

breasts" to "gall" in order to be unkind (47–48). This self-imposed malevolent version of maternity does not "unsex" (41) her but continues her mother-centered identity.

8. Harold Jenkins, the Arden editor of *Hamlet*, rightly argues that Hamlet's reaction to Ophelia is not explained by her refusal of his letters (pp. 149–50) or by Hamlet's discovery of Polonius behind the arras in the nunnery scene (note to 3.1.130–31 on p. 283, and a longer note on pp. 496–97). Hamlet's rejection of Ophelia proceeds from more deep-seated motives than such specific causation would indicate.

9. According to Stephen Greenblatt, Othello's

identity depends upon a constant performance, as we have seen, of his "story," a loss of his own origins, an embrace and a perpetual reiteration of the norms of another culture. It is this dependence that gives Othello, the warrior and alien, a relation to Christian values that is the existential equivalent of a religious vocation; he cannot allow himself the moderately flexible adherence that most ordinary men have toward their formal beliefs. Christianity is the alienating yet constitutive force in Othello's identity.

(*Renaissance Self-Fashioning: From More to Shakespeare* [Chicago: University of Chicago Press, 1980], p. 245)

10. On the issue of Venetian racism, Arthur Kirsch draws a sharper line than the evidence warrants between the specter of interracial sexuality Iago conjures up for Brabantio's benefit and the racially neutral emblems of black sin and white redemption promulgated by Christian idealism (*Shakespeare and the Experience of Love* [Cambridge: Cambridge University Press, 1981], pp. 19–21, 29–30). In support of a spiritual terminology of black and white that transcends race, Kirsch points to "evangelically tinted voyage literature, which treated inferior and black-faced foreigners as creatures whose innocence made them close to God and naturally prone to accept Christianity" (p. 20). But this attribution of "innocence" to "inferior and black-faced foreigners" is too close for comfort to colonializing condescension. In the specific context of *Othello*, a residual racism cannot be totally ruled out of Desdemona's remark: "I saw Othello's visage in his mind" (1.3.252). She means to praise Othello's mind, but a negative reflection on his actual black face lingers as one of the potential multiple effects of the line—for which Stephen Greenblatt lists three meanings, none of which can be excluded (*Renaissance Self-Fashioning*, p. 301 n. 30). The duke's less romantic translation of Desdemona's line more obviously adopts the strategy of excusing and circumventing Othello's literal blackness:

"If virtue no delighted beauty lack / Your son-in-law is far more fair than black" (1.3.289–90). Although the ocular proof of Othello's race is undeniable, his benefactor strives both to ignore and to compensate for it. This ethical praise depends on an uneasy blend of the two meanings of black as sin and race, and it is thus a praise that devalues Othello's racial identity in apologizing for it: he is good even though he is black.

11. Othello's image of housewives' travesty of his helmet recalls the mockery of the helmet and other implements of war in Botticelli's *Mars and Venus*. One does not have to see with the cynical eyes of Iago to realize that the painting represents more than the Neoplatonic allegory of *discordia concors* described by Edgar Wind in "Virtue Reconciled with Pleasure," in his *Pagan Mysteries in the Renaissance* (New York: W. W. Norton, 1968), pp. 81–96. The disparity between Venus's composure and Mars's loss of consciousness vividly evokes male fears of sexual union and the power it appears to give women over men. *Othello* gives far greater prominence to the "discordant element," the "sting" (p. 91), that Wind finds implicit in Botticelli's painting. The play does this by demythologizing the classical motif, translating it into tragic marital discord.

12. The recent interest in Shakespeare's representation of gender has produced a rich body of criticism on *Othello* that includes Shirley Garner, "Shakespeare's Desdemona," *Shakespeare Studies* 9 (1976): 233–52; Shirley Garner, "Male Bonding and the Myth of Women's Deception in Shakespeare's Plays," paper presented at the Northeast Modern Language Association convention in Quebec in 1981; Madelon Gohlke, " 'All that is spoke is marred': Language and Consciousness in *Othello*," *Women's Studies* 9 (1982): 157–76; Gayle Greene, " 'This That You Call Love': Sexual and Social Tragedy in *Othello*," *Journal of Women's Studies in Literature* 1 (1979): 16–32; Carol Thomas Neely, "Women and Men in *Othello*: 'What should such a fool / Do with so good a woman?' " *Shakespeare Studies* 10 (1977): 133–58; Edward A. Snow, "Sexual Anxiety and the Male Order of Things," *English Literary Renaissance* 10 (1980): 384–412; and Richard P. Wheeler, " 'and my loud crying still': The *Sonnets*, *The Merchant of Venice*, and *Othello*," in *Shakespeare's "Rough Magic": Essays in Honor of C. L. Barber*, ed. Peter Erickson and Coppélia Kahn (Newark, Del.: University of Delaware Press, 1985).

13. Rosalie Colie, "*Othello* and the Problematics of Love," in her *Shakespeare's Living Art* (Princeton: Princeton University Press, 1974), pp. 135–67.

14. Reuben A. Brower makes a similar point in *Hero and Saint: Shakespeare and the Graeco-Roman Heroic Tradition* (New York: Oxford University Press, 1971), pp. 6–7.

15. Othello's perception of the ideal Desdemona as the "fountain from which my current runs" (4.2.59) bodies forth the nurturant maternal breast, whereas his alienation redirects his imagination and swiftly converts the fountain into a disgusting image of the womb: "a cestern for foul toads / To knot and gender in" (4.2.61–62). The polarized images of fountain and cestern thus provide distinct physical locations for positive and negative male reactions to the female body, as in Lear's division between "women all above" and "down from the waist" (4.6.125,124). This division underlies Othello's split response between physical revulsion and sexual attraction in his subsequent speech:

> O ay, as summer flies are in the shambles,
> That quicken even with blowing. O thou weed!
> Who art so lovely fair and smell'st so sweet
> That the senses aches at thee, wouldst thou hadst never been born!
>
> (4.2.66-69)

In the effort to cancel Desdemona's image as "so lovely fair," he makes her a "weed" by focusing on her procreative capacity as the symbol of her impurity.

16. Desdemona's absolute commitment to "love him dearly" even "though he do shake me off / To beggarly divorcement" (4.2.157–58) provides a means for resolving the critical debate over whether she is submissive or active. Her response to the threat from Othello combines these two modes in a passive-aggressive response. She actively asserts her integrity, but this assertion is narrowly channeled into the cultural convention of female obedience and goodness. Ultimately, her goodness signifies both superiority and vengeance. Innocence has its own revenge, and Desdemona sets herself up in advance to take advantage of this revenge. The force of Desdemona's language in lines 156–61 bespeaks a defense whose effect is a revenge that turns "defeat" into victory: "And his unkindness may defeat my life, / But never taint my love" (160–61). In "Othello Unnamed," David Willbern points out that Desdemona's final utterance, while protecting Othello, simultaneously deprives him of identity (paper presented at the Modern Language Association convention in New York in 1981).

17. T. S. Eliot, "Shakespeare and the Stoicism of Seneca" (1927), in *Selected Essays*, p. 110. Reuben Brower is correct when he writes:

> The speech after he has been disarmed, almost certainly for the first time in his life, is of a kind never heard from Othello before. . . . The admission of defeat, that he is "not valiant," the renunciation of the epithet that was especially his, the questioning tone, and the lifeless echo of his old challenges, are all new.
>
> (*Hero and Saint*, p. 23)

However, Othello is unable to maintain this new tone. Brower is forced to deny the inconsistency and complexity of Othello's voice in the play's final scene because he overreacts against "the hard view of Othello" exemplified by Eliot and Leavis (ibid., p.2, n.1).

18. Ibid., p. 111.

19. Eliot, "Shakespeare and the Stoicism of Seneca," p. 111.

20. In "Shakespeare's Nothing," in *Representing Shakespeare*, pp. 244–63, David Willbern shows how the equation of "nothing" with the vagina operates in *King Lear*. If Lear has "nothing," he has female rather than male genitals.

21. In "*King Lear* and the Crisis of Patriarchy," a paper presented to the seminar on "Gender and Genre: Feminist Approaches to Shakespearean Roles" at the Shakespeare Congress in Stratford-on-Avon in 1981, Coppélia Kahn cites Lear's outburst—"O how this mother swells up toward my heart" (2.4.56)—as a starting point for her discussion of the play's use of the motif of the mother.

22. In "The Family in Shakespeare's Development: Tragedy and Sacredness," in *Representing Shakespeare*, pp. 188–202, C. L. Barber writes of Lear's prison speech: "But he still wants his daughter 'to love [her] father all.' A chasm of irony opens as we realize that he is leading her off to death. His vision of prison amounts, almost literally, to a conception of heaven on earth—*his* heaven, the 'kind nursery' after all" (p. 199).

23. Inga-Stina Ewbank, in "Shakespeare's Portrayal of Women: A 1970s View," in *Shakespeare: Pattern of Excelling Nature*, ed. David Bevington and Jay L. Halio (Newark, Del.: University of Delaware Press, 1978), pp. 222–29, asks two basic questions: "Is Shakespeare saying that women must be sacrificed in order that men may learn? And do they learn?" (p. 228). In the case of *King Lear*, her answer to both questions is yes, though she wonders whether the learning justifies the sacrifice: "In the tragedy that was to follow *Othello*, Lear does learn what Cordelia's

plain, literal language means; yet even he is left to die staring at her dead face" (p. 228). Ewbank overestimates the degree and scope of Lear's learning. The view that Cordelia is sacrificed but that Lear substantially does not learn more closely approximates our heart-rending experience of the play's "tough world" (5.3.315). Wilbur Sanders's observation about the concluding tone of "regret and pathos" is nearer the mark: "There is something faintly nerveless, if not unnerved, about the *Lear* accommodation of the unaccommodable" (Sanders and Howard Jacobson, *Shakespeare's Magnanimity* [New York: Oxford University Press, 1978], p. 81). But Sanders's comment has to be modified to apply to the characters rather than to the play. Lear, not *Lear*, makes the nerveless accommodation; the play shows us the unaccommodable and holds us to it.

24. In "The Last Tragic Heroes," in *Later Shakespeare*, ed. John Russell Brown and Bernard Harris (London: Edward Arnold, 1966), pp. 11–28, G. K. Hunter sets out "to complicate the relationship of *Lear* to the Last Plays by suggesting ways in which the group of 'Last Tragedies' acts as intermediary" (p. 11). I follow Hunter's lead by providing another account of how these intervening tragedies affect our sense of Shakespeare's development and especially our use of the connection between *King Lear* and *The Winter's Tale*, that is, between the Lear–Cordelia and the Leontes–Perdita bonds. Like Hunter, I find that "the Last Plays have to be greatly simplified before we can see them just as fables of reconciliation" (p. 28).

25. D. W. Harding, from whose cogent insights I have benefited, gives insufficient weight to the larger social context in "Women's Fantasy of Manhood: A Shakespearean Theme," *Shakespeare Quarterly* 20 (1969): 245–53. His title overstresses Lady Macbeth's role as an individual character, making her unduly responsible for the "fantasy of manhood," which the play presents as a culturewide problem. She tries to conform, as do other characters, to the prevailing cultural emphasis on the display of "manly readiness" and the suppression of "naked frailties" (2.3.126,133). Harding suggests that Macduff embodies "the most complex experience of manliness" in the play and comes closest to achieving the ideal of a masculine identity capable of balancing courage and sensitivity. On the contrary, Macduff fits the general pattern of distorted masculinity. The symbolic value attaching to his statement "But I must also feel it as a man" (4.3.221) is too slender a thread to withstand the dramatic action of Macduff's swift assent to Malcolm's "manly" revenge (235) and of his excessive violence in decapitating Macbeth (5.9.20–25). His appearance in the final scene does not offer an image of manhood on

which we can build much trust. The play comes full circle not because Duncan's goodness has been restored but because the violence on which Duncan depended continues—Macbeth's initial praiseworthy act of "fixing his head upon our battlements" (1.2.23) is echoed in Macduff's final triumph.

26. Harry Berger, Jr., makes this point in "The Early Scenes of *Macbeth:* Preface to a New Interpretation," *English Literary History* 47 (1980): 1–31.

27. Although Macbeth stifles awareness by "dying with harness on our back" (5.5.51) and although he distances himself from his own story by depersonalizing it ("It is a tale / Told by an idiot, full of sound and fury, / Signifying nothing" [5.5.26–28]), he gives poignant testimony to the bankruptcy of his commitment to "manly readiness." The relentless rhythm of the "Tomorrow, and to-morrow, and to-morrow" speech mimics the automaton identity to which such readiness can lead. Macbeth's summation brutally exposes his particular life, the empty "strutting and fretting" of his masculine role. Nonetheless, he is left with just enough "naked frailty"—the use of "almost" in "I have almost forgot the taste of fears" (9) makes a crucial qualification— to be permitted the integrity of "signifying" this "nothing."

4. IDENTIFICATION WITH THE MATERNAL IN *ANTONY AND CLEOPATRA*

1. Janet Adelman's is the best account of the issue of mixed genres in the play; see the sections "The Various World" and "Comic Perspectives" in Ch. 1 of *The Common Liar: An Essay on Antony and Cleopatra* (New Haven: Yale University Press, 1973), pp. 40–52.

2. Reuben A. Brower's comment on earlier renditions suggests that the lovers' mutuality is part of Shakespeare's design:

> Shakespeare had almost certainly read Daniel's *The Tragedy of Cleopatra,* and perhaps also the Countess of Pembroke's translation of Garnier, *The Tragedy of Antonie;* but he could not have found in these long-winded and relatively simple plays anything like a model for *Antony and Cleopatra.* The titles indicate a major difference from Shakespeare— neither author was capable of embracing the two dramas in a single vision.
>
> (*Hero and Saint: Shakespeare and the Graeco-Roman Heroic Tradition* [New York: Oxford University Press, 1971], p. 346)

3. Anne Barton brilliantly discusses the structure of *Antony and Cleopatra* in terms of the special "sense of an ending" produced by act 5 in " 'Nature's piece 'gainst fancy': The Divided

Catastrophe in *Antony and Cleopatra*" (Inaugural lecture, Bedford College, University of London, May 1973). In *Romeo and Juliet* the woman also survives the male hero, but so briefly that the effect is not comparable. Barton's account, however, needs to be qualified by reference to Linda Bamber's convincing argument in *Comic Women, Tragic Men: A Study of Gender and Genre in Shakespeare* (Stanford, Stanford University Press, 1981) that Cleopatra's prominence does not mean she has a dramatic weight precisely equivalent to Antony's. Despite Cleopatra's centrality, she is still more a perceived object than a perceiving agent: "But even as co-protagonist she is better understood as an Other than as a version of Self" (p. 12). The primacy of the male point of view prevents "an inside view of Cleopatra" (p. 55).

4. Phyllis Rackin makes this case with regard to Cleopatra in "Shakespeare's Boy Cleopatra, the Decorum of Nature, and the Golden World of Poetry," *PMLA*, 87 (1972): 201–12.

5. Robert B. Heilman's " 'Twere Best Not Know Myself': Othello, Lear, Macbeth," *Shakespeare 400*, ed. James G. McManaway (New York: Holt, Rinehart & Winston, 1964), pp. 89–98, is a useful study of the drama of self-knowledge. However, his sequel—"From Mine Own Knowledge: A Theme in the Late Tragedies," *Centennial Review* 8 (1964): 17–38—merely extrapolates the theme of self-knowledge to subsequent plays; the result is a dismissive reading of *Antony and Cleopatra*, in which preconceived expectations prevent significant engagement with the play on its own terms. Heilman notes the glibness of Antony's conventionally tragic self-regard but uses this perception to find fault with the play for not delivering a certain prescribed experience.

6. In literary-historical terms, the gender sharing represented in *Antony and Cleopatra* does not correspond to the sexual fusion Spenser portrays in the original ending of Book 3 of *The Faerie Queene*. One reason for Spenser's revision of this ending is the awareness that such an androgynous merger is too simplified; the entire interaction of Artegall and Britomart over the course of Books 3 through 5 is more adequate to the complexities of gender-role exchange.

7. Eugene M. Waith, *The Herculean Hero* (New York: Columbia University Press, 1962), pp. 113–21; and Maurice Charney, *Shakespeare's Roman Plays* (Cambridge: Harvard University Press, 1961), pp. 79–141.

8. In "The Mother of the World: A Psychoanalytic Interpretation of *Antony and Cleopatra*," *English Literary Renaissance* 7 (1977): 324–51, Constance Brown Kuriyama stresses the importance of "recognizing Cleopatra's maternal identity."

9. *Shakespeare's Plutarch,* ed. T. J. B. Spencer (Harmonds-worth: Penguin, 1964), p. 174.

10. Antony does not receive the chronicle he originally sought in his successful performance of "gests" (4.8.2) for Cleopatra during the brief second battle on land:

> If from the field I shall return once more
> To kiss these lips, I will appear in blood;
> I and my sword will earn our chronicle.
> There's hope in't yet.
>
> (3.13.173–76)

The soldier whom Cleopatra's eulogy memorializes is not the warrior of Antony's "former fortunes" (4.15.53) but the newly created erotic hero. Cleopatra's imagining of a gigantic Antony is mere deception if read literally as an image of military success, but it makes good sense as a metaphor of the lover's powerful impact. As Rosalie Colie suggests, Cleopatra's language involves a remetaphoring that "rejects conventional hyperbole and invents and creates new overstatements, new forms of overstatement" (*Shakespeare's Living Art* [Princeton: Princeton University Press, 1974], p. 198).

11. Robert Ornstein, "The Ethic of the Imagination: Love and Art in 'Antony and Cleopatra,' " in *Later Shakespeare: Stratford-Upon-Avon Studies 8,* ed. John Russell Brown and Bernard Harris (London: Edward Arnold, 1966), pp. 44–45. Ornstein uses Donne's "Canonization" to support his final view of *Antony and Cleopatra* yet ignores the limitations implied by the second half of the line "We can die by it, if not live by love" and by the adjective in "We'll build in sonnets pretty rooms."

12. Ibid. Ruth Nevo's "The Masque of Greatness," *Shakespeare Studies 3* (1967): 111–28, deftly shows how Cleopatra's art is related to the masque tradition and how the play's ending is organized as a counterpointing of Cleopatra's masque with Octavius's antimasque. However, this pattern of allusions to the masque form does not make the play itself a masque in any conventional sense. Rather, Shakespeare evokes the masque in order to turn it to tragic account. But the concerted reference to the masque in *Antony and Cleopatra* helps to distinguish its unremitting tragic mode from the style of earlier tragedies.

13. Heilman, "From Mine Own Knowledge," p. 28.

14. I agree with Derek Traversi's emphasis on the need for balancing perspectives in approaching this play. In the preface to his *Shakespeare: The Roman Plays* (Stanford: Stanford University

Press, 1963), he calls *Antony and Cleopatra* "possibly the greatest test of balanced Shakespeare criticism." Nonetheless, there are different ways to strike this balance. Traversi adopts a critical stance of controlled moderation that mutes both sides of the conflict he is arbitrating, with the result that he insufficiently speaks to the emotional extremes we actually experience.

15. C. L. Barber, *Shakespeare's Festive Comedy* (Princeton: Princeton University Press, 1959), p. 8. In *The Living Monument: Shakespeare and the Theatre of His Time* (Cambridge: Cambridge University Press, 1976), Muriel Bradbrook reports that Barber used "festive tragedy" to describe the play (p. 176).

5. THE LIMITATIONS OF REFORMED MASCULINITY IN *THE WINTER'S TALE*

1. Murray M. Schwartz established the patriarchal design of the play in two articles, "Leontes' Jealousy in *The Winter's Tale*," *American Imago* 30 (1973): 250–73; and "*The Winter's Tale*: Loss and Transformation," *American Imago* 32 (1975): 145–99.

2. Marcel Mauss's anthropological study, *The Gift*, trans. Ian Cunnison (New York: W. W. Norton, 1967), provides a useful context for this passage. As Mauss explains, giving—especially conspicuously displayed giving—is a means of establishing status and demonstrating power. Inability to repay or to give back at the same lavish rate places one lower down in the hierarchy. The lesser status feared by Archidamus and Polixenes cuts across the ideal image of "twinn'd lambs" (1.2.67) equal in love.

3. Ibid., p. 63.

4. In his introduction to Hesiod's *Theogony* (Indianapolis: Bobbs-Merrill, 1953), Norman O. Brown gives a pertinent exposition of the patriarchal structure that governs the Greek divinities under Zeus.

5. Edgar Wind, *Pagan Mysteries in the Renaissance* (New York: W. W. Norton, 1968), pp. 26–41, 113–21.

6. As Harry Berger, Jr., comments in "*King Lear*: The Lear Family Romance," *Centennial Review* 23 (1979): 348–76: "Lear runs away to escape from Cordelia but runs away to make her capture him again" (p. 367).

7. Sherry B. Ortner, "Is Female to Male as Nature Is to Culture?" in *Women, Culture, and Society*, ed. Michelle Zimbalist Rosaldo and Louise Lamphere (Stanford: Stanford University Press, 1974), pp. 67–87.

8. Wind, *Pagan Mysteries*, pp. 204–5.

9. The transition from the maternal nurturance associated with nature to patriarchal culture is echoed in the transformation wrought by Julio Romano, the purported creator of Hermione's statue, whose work "would beguile Nature of her custom, so perfectly is he her ape" (5.2.99–100). His may be "an art / That Nature makes" (4.4.91–92), but the use of "beguile" suggests the element of appropriation that lurks in artistic reverence for mother nature.

10. Myra Glazer Schotz's observations about *Pericles*—in "The Great Unwritten Story: Mothers and Daughters in Shakespeare," in *The Lost Tradition: Mothers and Daughters in Literature,* ed. Cathy N. Davidson and E. M. Broner (New York: Frederick Ungar, 1980), pp. 44–54—have greater pertinence for *The Winter's Tale* than she acknowledges. Of *Pericles* she comments: "In its Shakespearean context, however, this mother–daughter 'passion and rapture' is modified, reconceived as *sub species paternitatis*"—a formulation that "allows the male to retain control" (p. 50).

11. C. L. Barber, " 'Thou that beget'st him that did thee beget': Transformation in 'Pericles' and 'The Winter's Tale,' " *Shakespeare Survey* 22 (1969): 65–66. Barber's interpretation focuses on the removal of Leontes's homosexual attraction to Polixenes. But it is equally important to stress the ongoing contribution of their relationship once it is established on a new, nonsexual basis. Leontes retains a significant psychological and political investment in the tie to Polixenes, who can once again call him "Dear my brother" (5.3.53).

12. Virginia Woolf's belief in Shakespeare's androgyny exemplifies the problem. In *A Room of One's Own* (New York: Harcourt, Brace & World, 1957), Woolf comments: "Coleridge certainly did not mean, when he said that a great mind is androgynous, that it is a mind that has any special sympathy with women" (p. 102). Woolf severs the connection usually assumed between the androgynous male author and a "special sympathy with women" but does not sufficiently apply this insight to her appraisal of Shakespeare.

13. In "Miraculous Harp: A Reading of Shakespeare's *Tempest,*" *Shakespeare Studies* 5 (1969): 253–83, Harry Berger, Jr., makes a convincing case for the distinction between protagonist and dramatist: "Criticism of Shakespeare is actually, as I shall try to show, Shakespeare's criticism of Prospero" (p. 280). However, in *The Winter's Tale*, no sharp distinction between Shakespeare and Leontes can be maintained in the final scene. Some aspects of male gratification are less accessible in *The Winter's*

Tale because Shakespeare himself may be indulging in them; hence, criticism of Shakespeare is relevant in this instance.

14. A comparison of *The Comedy of Errors* with *The Winter's Tale* is useful here. Both plays enact family reunions, whose culmination is the unexpected appearance of the mother figure who is both sacred and secular. The ending of the early comedy does seem too neatly symmetrical and is subject to the charge of theatrical sleight of hand. The late romance, by contrast, has a degree of emotional depth that counteracts the idea that the play's conclusion is sheer artifice. The strength of *The Winter's Tale* comes from its integrating in a single couple the marital turbulence and familial rejoicing that in *The Comedy of Errors* are disconnected because the romantic theme of parental separation and reunion (Egeon and Aemilia) is split off from the farcical realism of everyday marital trouble represented by Antipholus of Ephesus and Adriana.

15. Maynard Mack, "Engagement and Detachment in Shakespeare's Plays," *Essays on Shakespeare and Elizabethan Drama in Honor of Hardin Craig*, ed. Richard Hosley (Columbia: University of Missouri Press, 1962), pp. 275–96.

16. T. S. Eliot, "John Ford" (1932), in *Selected Essays: 1917–1932* (New York: Harcourt, Brace, 1932), pp. 170–71.

Index

Compositor: Huron Valley Graphics
Text: Palatino
Display: Palatino
Printer: Braun-Brumfield, Inc.
Binder: Braun-Brumfield, Inc.